Brasenose College, Oxford, in the eighteenth century. Original copper engraving
by Pierre Van Der Aa in the possession of Phinizy Spalding.

Oglethorpe:
A Brief Biography

Oglethorpe:
A Brief Biography

Amos Aschbach Ettinger

edited with an introduction by
Phinizy Spalding

This Essay was awarded
the Beit Prize in Colonial History for 1929
at the University of Oxford.

MERCER
MUP

ISBN 0-86554-110-8

All books published by Mercer University Press
are produced on acid-free paper that exceeds
the minimum standards set by the National Historical
Publications and Records Commission.

Library of Congress Cataloging in Publication Data:
Ettinger, Amos Aschbach, 1901-1969
Oglethorpe, a brief biography.

"This essay was awarded the Beit Prize in Colonial History for 1929 at the University of Oxford."

Includes bibliographical references.

1. Oglethorpe, James Edward, 1696-1785. 2. Georgia—History—Colonial period, ca. 1600-1775. 3. Georgia—Governors—Biography. I. Spalding, Phinizy. II. Title.

F289.037E87 1984   975.8'02'0924 [B]   84-8403

ISBN 0-86554-110-8 (alk. paper)

Contents

To Kathryn Gable Ettinger

Introduction

"A gorgeous sight to stand on deck in the early dawn and see the haze lift gently, as the boat slowly creeps up the Thames . . . where at King George V Docks, we are to land." So wrote, on 13 September 1926, the twenty-five year old Amos Aschbach Ettinger, college graduate, aspiring Oxonian, and future biographer of James Edward Oglethorpe.[1] His passage from America on the *Carmania* had been relaxing and uneventful; he had spent his time reading, sleeping, and eating the excellent shipboard food. The Scilly Isles had been sighted on the afternoon of 11 September and, after stopping briefly at LeHavre and enjoying a clear Sunday in the English Channel—"made famous," said Ettinger, "by 'Trudie' Ederle and the Armada"—the ship slowly wound its way up the river toward London. After taking a train to Liverpool Street station in the heart of the old city, Ettinger taxied to the mammoth pile that was the Russell Hotel in Russell Square. On the following day he left for Oxford, the "goal of my ambitions."[2]

---

[1]Amos Aschbach Ettinger, "The Diary of an American Oxonian," 9, in possession of Mrs. A. A. Ettinger of Fenton, Michigan. Xerox copy in the Ettinger Collection, Rare Books and Manuscripts Division, University of Georgia Library. Hereinafter cited as Ettinger, "Diary." Used with the permission of Mrs. Ettinger. Unless otherwise stipulated, unpublished letters, records of interviews, and the like can be found in the Amos Aschbach Ettinger Collection, housed in Rare Books and Manuscripts Division, University of Georgia Library, Athens.

[2]Ettinger, "Diary," 4, 5, 7-8.

Amos Aschbach Ettinger was the son and only child of George Taylor Ettinger and Emma Aschbach, both of whom came from distinguished Pennsylvania "Dutch" families. The elder Ettinger received his undergraduate and master's degrees from Muhlenberg College in Allentown, Pennsylvania, the place of his birth. In 1891 he was awarded the Ph.D. by New York University and returned to Allentown to teach at Muhlenberg where he spent the rest of his life. In addition to holding many community posts, Amos's father was also the first president of the Allentown Library Association from 1912 until 1943, was one-time president of the Lehigh Valley Historical Society, and was often a delegate to various Lutheran conferences held in the state. In 1892 Ettinger became professor of pedagogy and associate professor of Latin at Muhlenberg. In 1917 he was made professor of the Latin language and literature, a position he held until his retirement in 1937.

In addition to his teaching responsibilities, George Ettinger was the college's first dean in 1904. At his own request he retired from this post in 1931. Amos's father published a number of books, was keenly interested in fine buildings and in collecting rare coins and stamps, and was an ardent proponent of the salutary impact of local history upon a community. He had the reputation of being an excellent teacher whose particular favorite among Latin authors was Horace.

The Ettinger family (George Taylor's father was named Amos) had been in the Lehigh County area of Pennsylvania since the eighteenth century and had consistently married other German families in the neighborhood. Emma, George's wife, was also a native of Allentown and daughter of the architect, Gustavus Adolphus Aschbach.[3] So it comes as no surprise to discover that Amos Aschbach Ettinger, who was born in Allentown on 24 May 1901, grew up in a closely knit household

---

[3]The information that was used in this section was drawn from *Who Was Who in America*, 2 (1950), 178; *The National Cyclopaedia of American Biography*, 37 (New York: James T. White & Company, 1951) 388-89; Robert Horn, unpublished manuscript, "Muhlenberg College: History of 100 Years, 1848-1948," in the Muhlenberg College Library, and *The History of Lehigh County, Pennsylvania* (1914) 319-23. The author would like particularly to thank Richard C. Shollenberger of the Muhlenberg College Library for his help in this regard.

whose priorities rated history, reading, and music high among the most important things in life. Their home was a warmly affectionate one where ideas and beauty were emphasized—a sheltered and loving oasis from the outside world of politics and finance. Amos's intellectual growth was dominated by his parents' concepts of aesthetics and values. The son's training at home must surely have done as much as anything to lead him into the field of scholarship.

Amos took his A.B. at Muhlenberg in 1921.[4] When nearing completion of his undergraduate work Ettinger—whose interests had already turned toward history—applied unsuccessfully for a Rhodes Scholarship.[5] Following this disappointment the young man attended the University of Pennsylvania and received an A.M. in 1923. Concentrating on American diplomatic history, he continued his research in 1923-1924 as a graduate student at Pennsylvania where he also served as an assistant in history. He moved on to Lafayette College where he was instructor in history from 1924 to 1926.[6] His involvement in scholarship deepened, so he applied for admission and was accepted at Brasenose College, Oxford.

Oxford in those days did not ordinarily accept American students other than Rhodes scholars, but Ettinger's record was strong enough to permit him to enroll at Brasenose as an undergraduate. (His master's degree from Pennsylvania had no standing with the Oxford officials.) So he was accepted on the same footing there as were the young matriculants fresh out of Eton, Harrow, or Charterhouse.[7] This was the same young American who watched so intently as his ship made its way up the

---

[4]*Directory of American Scholars*, ed. Jaques Cattell, 3d ed. (New York: R. R. Bowker Co., 1957) 221.

[5]Amos Aschbach Ettinger to James Lowry Clifford, ca. mid-March 1937, letter quoted with the kind permission of Professor Clifford.

[6]*Directory of American Scholars*, 221; Ettinger, "Diary," 1; *The Revista* (Moravian College Yearbook, 1939) 15.

[7]Personal interview with Leonard Hector, 20 June 1973, at the Public Record Office (PRO), London. Hector, as will become clear in the narrative, was a classmate and friend of Ettinger during his stay at Brasenose.

Thames, who railed in his "Diary" against the train to Liverpool Station—"slow as a snail"—and who waited so impatiently for 14 September 1926, the day he was to report to Brasenose College, to come.[8]

On 14 September Ettinger went up to Oxford from London and began to accustom himself to the routine of Brasenose—affectionately called BNC—and the city. He made arrangements for rooms with the Harold Drews on Edith Road. The Drews, in fact, became Ettinger's English family, and he even stood as godfather to one of their children. In their home he was able to find the kind of associations, diversions, and ties of affection that he would otherwise have missed even more acutely than he did. Drew was employed at Brasenose and presumably Ettinger was recommended to him by the college officials. Whatever the situation, the relationship between the American and his English family blossomed from the first and was to last throughout the lifetime of the principals involved.

As he familiarized himself with the college and town Ettinger tried to see Professor Robert McNutt McElroy, who later became Ettinger's scholarly mentor during his Oxford stay, but McElroy was not expected back until the beginning of the term. Whereupon Ettinger, a confirmed theatergoer, returned to London and attended a "shilling shocker" entitled "The Ghost Town" that same night.[9] Two days later Ettinger received his final permit to work in the British Public Record Office. The European and British phases of his research into the diplomatic records of the mission of Pierre Soulé to Spain in the 1850s, which would result in Ettinger's first book-length publication, began soon thereafter. Ettinger the scholar and researcher "enjoyed the preliminaries exceedingly," just as Ettinger the playgoer and music lover spent most of his time in London attending plays and concerts.[10]

On 11 October he left the big city for Oxford and the new term, collected his books, went to his Edith Road rooms (of which he highly approved), and enjoyed a good night's sleep in his "Wonderfully soft

---

[8]Ettinger, "Diary," 7.

[9]Ibid., 11.

[10]Ibid., 14, 16, 17.

bed."[11] On the following morning Ettinger was up at 8 A.M. and had breakfast thirty minutes later in his own living room where he had a coal fire provided against the rainy day and a good gas light "for reading." He went to the college to attend to various matters, returned "home" for lunch, and had his evening meal in BNC's dining hall. Quickly he established a pattern of reading, studying, and attending functions at BNC that was to characterize his stay throughout the academic year 1926-1927. At last, on 16 October, he met Professor McElroy and under his guidance Amos Aschbach Ettinger the historian began to emerge.[12]

Robert McNutt McElroy, staunch advocate of Anglo-American ties and friendship, was at the time Harold Vyvyan Harmsworth Professor of American History in Oxford, having succeeded Samuel Eliot Morison, the first Harmsworth professor, in 1925. A native of Kentucky, McElroy took three degrees from Princeton, studied in Europe, and succeeded Woodrow Wilson as chairman of Princeton's department of history and political science in 1912. He is usually considered to have been America's first exchange professor to China, serving there in 1916-1917. Prior to 1926, he was best known for *The Winning of the Far West* (1914), *The Representative Idea in History* (1917), and a life of Grover Cleveland that appeared in 1923. His opinions on Anglo-American unity and his notion that "the enemy of the world is the provincial mind" probably had a dramatic impact on the impressionable and rather naive young American.[13] Ettinger wrote of McElroy: "He is an inspiration to any student. Tall, well-built, keen, friendly, helpful and kind, he wins one's immediate confidence." He was the sort of person "for whom you can work your head off."[14] And all but work it off Ettinger did. He was, however, anxious for the kind of goad McElroy provided. As he put it, his "dream was at last realized. I am now a member in good standing of the ancient, illustrious and honorable University of Oxford"

---

[11]Ibid., 26.

[12]Ibid., 26-8.

[13]*Who's Who in America*, 1918-1919, 10, 1824; ibid., 1950-1951, 26, 1818; *New York Times*, 17 January 1959, 19.

[14]Ettinger, "Diary," 28.

and of BNC. "I feel at home already here," Ettinger wrote on 18 October, "A great place to work."[15]

Actually Ettinger, who had visited Oxford several years prior to 1926, was not completely unfamiliar with the city and its university. Still, being an official part of the academic community was exhilarating, and it became even more so when he commenced research in the various archival depositories and libraries scattered throughout the city. He enjoyed his research immensely, and the work on Pierre Soulé, which he had begun at Pennsylvania, looked most promising to McElroy. At the latter's insistence, Ettinger began to "write up what he had" while, at the same time, researching into newspapers and diplomatic documents to which he had no access in America. After a series of consultations Ettinger was informed that if he could "make good on the B. Litt., they will accept Soulé's life for the D. Phil."[16] His aim then would be accomplished; he would have his doctorate in hand and, as his father had done with such distinction and honor, Ettinger would be well along the road to his goal of becoming a college professor.

With his life's aim spelled out, Ettinger set to work to complete as much of his research and writing on Soulé as he could before returning to America in the spring of 1927. He adopted a rigid schedule that was rarely interrupted, and then only for good reason. His entire Christmas break, which ran from 11 December through 19 January, was spent in London at the Public Record Office and the British Museum. Although he enjoyed plays and concerts in the evenings and on weekends, it was a lonely time for the young man. On Christmas Day, in fact, after attending morning services in St. Paul's, he was unable even to buy a newspaper or find a restaurant open. Finally in the evening he had a dinner of roast turkey and Christmas pudding. Still, it was "a mean kind of a Christmas Day. Believe me, the next one I spend AT HOME."[17]

---

[15]Ibid., 29, 30.

[16]Ibid., 32, 33.

[17]Ibid., 50-65, for his London Christmas. The quotation is taken from ibid., 57.

By 2 March 1927, Ettinger wrote that he could see the end of his efforts on Soulé in view, but still had work to do in the Paris archives. His stay in the French city, which he disliked, and the Bibliotheque Nationale, which he found "hard and lonely to work in," lasted less than a week.[18] Returning to Britain, he tidied up loose ends in London and Oxford, attended a sporting match or two, bade a sad farewell to the Drews, and sailed for America aboard the *Leviathan* on 29 March.[19]

Ettinger's life during his relatively brief stay in Oxford during 1926 and 1927 hardly conformed to Evelyn Waugh's *Brideshead Revisited* stereotype. He was basically a shy and retiring man among those he did not know well; he prospered primarily upon study and routine. Friends he made but slowly at Brasenose, possibly because he was considerably older than the undergraduates with whom he was grouped. Still, he found them "good chaps," albeit somewhat reserved.

Brasenose had a reputation at the time for being a school that gave an athlete more than just an even break. Ettinger, who was too big a man physically—perhaps as large as eighteen stone—to take part successfully in athletics, was an avid follower of English rugby and soccer. But he never understood, reminisced one of his school friends, the aesthetics of cricket.[20] American football was his passion and he waited patiently all during the fall of 1926 to receive word, usually through a cable from his father, how Muhlenberg's team fared of a Saturday. He was particularly depressed on 18 September. "This afternoon I miss the first opening football game at home in 16 years. Even the beautiful sunshine we have had all the week doesn't help much to cheer me up, when I think of that."[21]

Gradually, though, he got over his homesickness and made a few good friends. One day when Ettinger was caught at the college by an

---

[18]Ibid., 83-9.

[19]Ibid., 90-6.

[20]Interview with Donald Tyerman, 8 June 1973. Tyerman, who was at BNC with Ettinger, later became editor of *The Economist*. See *The International Who's Who, 1980-81* (London, 1980) 1295.

[21]Ettinger, "Diary," 16.

unexpected shower of rain, Leonard C. Hector, a freshman from Bristol, offered him shelter. The two young men began eating their evening meals together at the college, and on 19 October Hector asked Ettinger, whom his Oxford friends called Mose, up to his room to play mahjongg. "As I live out of college," he wrote, "I had to leave by 9:15 before the gates close, or I couldn't get out."[22] He also met and established friendships with fellow students Donald Tyerman and J. K. Creer. They discovered they had much in common, particularly an interest in studies—a trait that set them apart in the BNC of the 1920s. Furthermore, none of the three Englishmen was an athlete or a graduate of a public school. According to Tyerman, loneliness and a need for a social outlet brought the four together, and they enjoyed one year, at least, of very "intense companionship." After that time they tended to drift apart as their interests diverged.[23] Originally Ettinger and his friends suffered from grave misconceptions about each other, remarked Hector. Mose thought that his new English associates were typical undergraduates; in their turn, the Englishmen thought Ettinger the stereotypical American graduate student.[24] At twenty-five and with grim determination to finish his work and proceed to an academic career, Ettinger reflected the sort of high seriousness not often found in the American graduate student of the 1920s. On their part Creer, Tyerman, and Hector in no way reflected the blasé pseudosophistication that was characteristic of many Oxonians during the same period. Once they overcame their misconceptions—a process that did not take long—the four men of BNC settled down to a fruitful and pleasant relationship.

On 3 November Ettinger noted: "In afternoon entertained Hector, Creer, and Tyerman, 3 scholars of BNC, in a Mah Jongg party. They all thanked me profusely, and said they had a good time. I know I did."[25] Thus began something of a tradition. Virtually every weekend the four-

---

[22]Interview with Leonard C. Hector, 20 June 1973, PRO; Ettinger, "Diary," 35.

[23]Tyerman interview, 7 June 1973.

[24]Hector interview, 20 June 1973.

[25]Ettinger, "Diary," 37.

some met at Mose's room and played cards or, more often, mah-jongg. They ate fish and chips, drank cider, and munched throughout on peppermint creams. The fish and chips were Mose's treat; he also provided "the fags."[26]

His old friends remember Ettinger as a very simple man who liked to let off steam by being boisterous. He also resorted to harmless practical jokes and atrocious puns. He liked horseplay and "primitive wrestling," which endeared him to the Drew boys with whom he loved to tussle. Hector saw Ettinger as he saw Theodore Roosevelt—as "a very large teddy bear."[27] Ettinger enjoyed teasing Creer by calling him "Ignatz." There was, Creer said, a cutting side to his humor as well the innocent.[28]

There were also hidden depths to Ettinger. He could follow the full score of an opera and hear the music in his mind. He loved Gilbert and Sullivan, but it was to Richard Wagner that his first loyalties went. He attended the weekly Wagner concerts when he was in London during the 1926-1927 season and commented upon their quality in his diary. And in Oxford one of his favorite pastimes, when he was not working, was studying the scores of Wagnerian operas.[29] At one point Ettinger took Hector's harmonica and played it for hours without becoming bored. The harmonica in those days denoted "plebeian associations," but as long as it was a musical instrument Mose did not care.[30]

But over and above all the incidentals, what came through to Mose's friends and to the reader of his diary was the serious student. To Tyerman, in spite of the friendliness and warmth that Ettinger radiated, it was always the scholar who dominated. "The Public Record Office was his temple, and his skedool [*sic*] of work was his bible." Still he loved "to laugh and to joke, in the simplest, most natural fashion, with-

---

[26]Interview with J. K. Creer, 20 June 1973. Ettinger himself did not smoke.

[27]Hector interview; Tyerman interview.

[28]Creer interview.

[29]See, for example, "Diary," 62.

[30]Hector interview.

out inhibition or much sophistication when he was with us youngsters."[31]
He seemed to work all day, every day, recalled Hector, and was surrounded in his quarters by "reams of typed stuff" when he was writing
his book on Soulé. Hector remembered his "almost insatiable appetite
for sweet things," particularly the ubiquitous peppermint creams. His
friend reflected that Mose was a "mighty trencherman for other food as
well."[32]

Ettinger made few friends outside this small group who, in addition to the Drews and their three sons, virtually made up his "circle" in
Oxford. But they were quite enough. With his work, his music, and his
interest in the stage, Ettinger, although missing his home in Pennsylvania, was really quite happy during his stay at BNC in 1926-1927 and
subsequently when he returned to finish work on his doctorate.

In 1930 Ettinger received the coveted D. Phil from Oxford University,[33] and two years later, after additional research and revision, his
book on Soulé was published by the Yale University Press. Entitled *The
Mission to Spain of Pierre Soulé, 1853-1855: A Study in the Cuban Diplomacy of the United States*, his conscientious labor was rewarded with the
John H. Dunning Prize by the American Historical Association at its
annual meeting in December 1933, "as the best book of 1931-33 in
American history."[34] His work in Oxford, which had produced the
Soulé book and the American Historical Association award, also won
Ettinger the distinguished Alexander Medal, given by the Royal Historical Society in 1930. In this case his winning essay concerned a proposed treaty in 1852 between France, Britain, and the United States to
assure Cuba to Spain.[35] The Soulé work was accepted as his thesis for

---

[31]Donald Tyerman to the author, 14 February 1973.

[32]Hector interview.

[33]Brasenose College Register, BNC Archives, Oxford.

[34]"Urbana Meeting, American Historical Association," *American Historical Review* 39 (April 1934): 441; Ettinger to the Bursar [A. D. Grant] of Brasenose College, 5 January 1934, BNC Archives.

[35]Brasenose College Register, BNC Archives; *Who's Who in America*, 1950-1951,
820. This essay was later incorporated into the Soulé book.

the D. Phil. in 1930, but by that time Ettinger's main research interests had shifted from nineteenth-century diplomacy and politics to eighteenth-century English philanthropy and colonization. The charitable movement that began to absorb his thinking and his time led Ettinger ultimately to a full consideration of the founding of Georgia in 1733 by James Edward Oglethorpe.

Given the sources, it is impossible to document precisely what influences worked on Ettinger after 1926-1927 to turn his interests to British colonial history. A likely explanation is that McElroy, who was in residence at Oxford as Harmsworth Professor for more than ten years after Ettinger first met him, was at least partly responsible for his student's shift in interest. McElroy's position on Anglo-American cooperation was well known, as was his admiration for the British Empire. He and Ettinger spent many hours consulting, organizing, and piecing together the thesis on Soulé. It is unthinkable that McElroy could not have had a major impact upon his student, although proof is lacking that he was the decisive force leading Ettinger to Oglethorpe.[36]

It may be, too, that Lawrence Henry Gipson, one of the preeminent colonial historians of the twentieth century, who came to Lehigh University in 1924 as head of the department of history and government, influenced Ettinger as he did so many other scholars. Although Ettinger was not officially affiliated with Lehigh until 1936, there were a number of intimate ties between small colleges in Pennsylvania—such as Lafayette, Moravian, Muhlenberg, and Lehigh—that would make such a supposition not illogical. Gipson, involved with his major work, *The British Empire before the American Revolution*, must have been available for advice as Ettinger completed the American phase of his Oglethorpe research in the early 1930s.

As likely to have had an impact on Ettinger as Gipson or even McElroy was the general mood surrounding Oxford. England was in economic distress in the 1920s and 1930s, but the intellectual atmosphere in the university town was still one of ebullience. The Empire, which stretched across the globe, was the country's pride and glory. In

---

[36]*New York Times*, 17 January 1959.

many ways epitomizing that Empire were the Rhodes Scholarships for which Ettinger had tried unsuccessfully. Even though he had lost in this competition it is apparent from his own writings that his admiration for these scholars, who represented what seemed to be the best America had to offer in both academics and sports, was enormous.

Also on the scene was the Beit chair in the history of the British Commonwealth, endowed in 1905 by Alfred Beit, staunch imperialist, diamond magnate, philanthropist, and close associate of Cecil Rhodes. Ettinger must have felt himself surrounded by examples of the greatness of the Empire. How logical, then, to turn to the history of one of the eighteenth-century founders of that system—James Oglethorpe—a man whose imperial vision, in Ettinger's mature assessment, looked ultimately toward a sort of loose union wherein England and her colonies could comfortably coexist. And how logical, too, when researching and writing for his biography, to offer his evolving piece on Oglethorpe in the competition for the Beit Prize, an award made annually through the university "for 'an essay on some subject connected with the history of the British Empire or the British Commonwealth.' " It was for the Beit honor that Ettinger set his cap in 1928-1929.[37]

But the most likely explanation of how Ettinger became interested in Oglethorpe relates directly to his earlier research. During his work on Soulé, Ettinger became attracted to the British antislavery movement and to the figure of William Wilberforce, whose labors to outlaw the institution in the Empire were finally successful in the 1830s. Ettinger's curiosity as to the causation of the movement led him to the Quaker criticisms of slavery and to the writings of Alexander Pope, Samuel Johnson, and Hannah More—all of them acquainted with Oglethorpe. Ultimately Ettinger went back to "the prohibition by James Oglethorpe of negro slavery in the new colony of Georgia," and he concluded that Oglethorpe's slavery ban, along with the efforts of Johnson, More, and others, "paved the way for William Wilberforce." So it seems likely that the historian approached his study of Georgia's founder through Ogle-

-----

[37]E. G. Collieu to the author, 10 January 1973; *The Dictionary of National Biography*, Supplement, January 1901-December 1911, (Oxford, 1912) 1: 128. The full sketch of Beit's life is found in ibid., 127-29.

thorpe's effort to prevent slavery from being established in his new province.[38]

Ettinger continued his close associations at BNC through 1929 as both his scholarship and his judgment matured. In addition to being staunchly German-American and Lutheran in his preferences, he also became an even more devoted Anglophile than he had been earlier. He loved the British Museum and a little restaurant (Schmidt's) nearby where he ate wiener schnitzel; he ingested the plays and the music that the city offered, at the same time deploring its dirty streets. And he developed a lifelong attachment to Oxford and its countryside. As he was returning to America in 1927, he had a final evening with the Drews. After their meal all of them walked to a rural area outside town where the Drews had a garden. "Old England in the spring twilight, with a church bell tolling in the distance. Beautiful beyond words. A fitting end to my stay in England."[39] It was to this area that he took his bride in 1938 because of its pleasant associations, but also because it "reminded him of the Lehigh Valley—our home."[40]

Unfortunately, Ettinger did not keep a diary to cover his Oxford experiences after March 1927. What is known of his life there, other than a few bare essentials, is sketchy at best. He was registered at BNC through the Lenten term of 1930; lived with the Drews during the entire period of his English stay; received his D. Phil. *in absentia* in June 1930; taught at Yale 1930-1931; and was back in England researching his life of Oglethorpe in 1932, 1933, and 1934.[41] The biography was finally published in 1936 and, to date, has remained the standard volume on the full career of Georgia's founder.[42] No less an authority than

---

[38]Amos Aschbach Ettinger, *The Mission to Spain of Pierre Soulé, 1853-1855: A Study in the Cuban Diplomacy of the United States* (Yale, 1932) 9.

[39]Ettinger, "Diary," 94-5.

[40]Mrs. Ettinger to author, 21 March 1974.

[41]See particularly BNC Archives; *Directory of American Scholars*, 3d ed., 150; *Who's Who in America*, 1950-1951, 820.

[42]Amos Aschbach Ettinger, *James Edward Oglethorpe, Imperial Idealist* (Oxford, 1936) 100-102 passim.

Ettinger himself said that the completed biography "gradually evolved" from the Beit Prize Essay,[43] but it has never been published. It would seem fortuitous that Thomas Gamble, onetime Savannah mayor and history enthusiast, heard of Ettinger's victory in this competition, wrote the author in 1929, and ultimately secured from him two copies of the essay, one of which went to the Research Section of the Savannah Public Library.[44] It was from this copy that the present writer, when researching his own volume on Oglethorpe, secured a photocopy that is used here to bring the Beit essay to the present readers.

The work that follows this introduction is the fruit of Amos Aschbach Ettinger's early research into the life of Oglethorpe. The essay is lengthy, as essays go, but short as books go. It possesses the weaknesses of a not yet fully developed historical framework and is flawed in some of its claims as well as in some of its assumptions. And yet at the same time, the essay is valuable in that it is a condensed version of the 1936 biography—a book that some of the reviewers found too long, too ambitious in its claims for Oglethorpe, and dotted with rambling and unrelated digressions that did not enhance the end product.[45] The essay, although youthful, is nonetheless more restrained in some of its interpretations than the full biography that followed it seven years later. And mercifully the author spares his reader the tedious recounting of genealogies of Oglethorpes past, which takes up roughly the first fifty pages of the 1936 volume.

One of many values that the essay has is that Ettinger's theories, especially those relating to Oglethorpe as an imperial idealist, stand out more clearly than they did in the final biography. As is so often the case even in works of fiction or criticism, the interpretations of an author

---

[43]Ettinger, *Oglethorpe*, vii.

[44]*Savannah Morning News*, 29 September 1929.

[45]For assessments that score the biography on these and other points see Verner Crane's review in the *American Historical Review* 42 (October 1936), 145-7; James Truslow Adams's piece in the *Saturday Review of Literature*, 22 February 1936, 25; and Nathan G. Goodman's critique in the *New York Times Book Review*, 22 March 1936, 4.

often emerge from the body of a shorter and less sophisticated work more readily than they do from a full study. Such is the case in relation to this preliminary treatment of the life of the founder of the colony of Georgia.

The essay is not without errors in fact as well as eccentricities in judgment. For example, war with Spain was not declared in 1737 but in 1739; the Georgia charter did not automatically revert to the king in 1752; Ettinger's claims for Oglethorpe's religious contributions are overdrawn; and so on. But the quibbles are minor. The study, just as everything that Ettinger ever published, is based upon extensive research that, by 1936, included a great deal more work in the contemporary newspapers. But the major theses that appeared in the final version of the published biography, particularly the themes of Oglethorpe's philanthropic and imperialistic motivations, are here to be seen in their first and most direct forms.

The present editor has interfered with the original text in only one particular. The footnotes in the original are numbered consecutively page by page. Because the present publication does not correspond to the pagination of the Beit Prize Essay as it was first typed, it was thought best to number the notes consecutively throughout a chapter rather than by each individual page. Footnote form, however, has been left as it was in 1929.

Ettinger divided his work into five unequal chapters, and the present writer has permitted this division to remain. In a brief introduction the author mentions the value of embarking upon such a study just as Georgia began to consider how best to celebrate its upcoming bicentennial in 1933. He also made bold to claim that Oglethorpe was "deserving of a modern Boswell," after which he launched into the heart of the matter. Ettinger's first chapter, a very brief one, is devoted to family background and is followed, in chapter two, by a treatment of the Jacobite activities of the Oglethorpes. Chapter three treats Oglethorpe's parliamentary career and attempts to put him in proper historical context. But it is the fourth chapter, which comprises more than half the entire piece, where the real value of this publication will be found. The origin, settlement, administration, and protection of the colony of Georgia by its founders are clearly spelled out; the three separate phases of Oglethorpe's career in America as Ettinger sees them—the administrative, the religious, and the military—are outlined. The last chapter deals with Oglethorpe's life in England following his final return in 1743 and is brief and to the point.

Many original sources and thousands of books that have a bearing on Oglethorpe, Georgia, and Hanoverian England have surfaced since the Beit Prize was awarded to Ettinger in 1929. But although it has been over half a century since this essay was so honored, it maintains its vitality and its relevance. Like Verner W. Crane's *The Southern Frontier*, originally published a year before the Beit Prize was awarded, and not unlike James Ross McCain's *Georgia as a Proprietary Province*, which is even older, there is a facet to Ettinger's writings on Oglethorpe that renders his judgments classic in their own field. Furthermore the essay sports a certain writing style that sets it apart from the humdrum. It is not like a typical American graduate school exercise—bland, colorless, dull, indecisive—but is more kin to the craft of the English historians of an earlier era. In addition, Ettinger must certainly have been influenced by McElroy, Andrews, Gipson, and others who considered good composition an art unto itself. However, the matured style of the published biography—complex, mildly ironic, occasionally flecked with humor—goes well beyond the essay. English usage, as is to be expected, abounds in both.

Although there were a number of things that Ettinger was never able to discover about Oglethorpe, his research that preceded the 1936 publication was so deep, particularly in the newspapers and the secondary sources, that he could feel sure he had missed little of substantial importance that was available at the time. With this kind of self-confidence Ettinger was secure in his judgments. Although this mature security is not so apparent in the essay, it is one of the factors that has helped the full-length biography stand the test of time.

The essay that follows this introduction is cut from the same cloth. In any sort of summing up that someone must make someday, what historian could ask more of posterity?

During Georgia's bicentennial celebration in 1933 Amos Ettinger served as special lecturer at Oglethorpe University in Atlanta, from which school he received an honorary degree in recognition of his work on the state's founder. Ettinger married Kathryn Gable in 1938 while filling the post of associate professor at Lehigh, a position he left in the following year to become professor and head of the history department at Moravian College, also located in Bethlehem. After a two-year stay at Moravian he moved back to Lehigh, did war work with Bethlehem Steel Company, and from 1946-1948 was visiting professor of history at Temple University. From 1948-1955 Ettinger engaged in research that he hoped would lead to the publication of a book in the Rivers of America Series, but his manuscript on the history of the Lehigh River was never completed and rests now among the collections of the Lehigh Valley Historical Society.

In 1955-1956 Ettinger was visiting professor of history at Southern Methodist University, but circulatory illnesses that related to a recently diagnosed diabetic condition caused him to be hospitalized and resulted in the amputation of a leg. The Ettingers and their son George moved to Michigan for Amos's convalescence and there he held his last academic position—professor of history at Flint (Michigan) Junior College. From 1958 until his death in November 1969 he and his family lived quietly in Fenton, Michigan, where his widow, son, and grandchildren still reside.

Phinizy Spalding

Acknowledgements

I have incurred a number of debts in writing the introduction to this Beit Prize Essay. My appreciation goes to the librarians and archivists of Muhlenberg and Moravian Colleges and of Lehigh University who helped me follow Amos Aschbach Ettinger during his career as student and teacher. Richard C. Shollenberger at Muhlenberg should be especially singled out. At Brasenose College, Oxford, Mr. E. G. Collieu not only responded to my queries about the school in the 1920s, but he also went into the archives in order to make my work there easier. During my visit to Oxford in the summer of 1973 his hospitality was welcomed and thoroughly appreciated.

Of former colleagues of Dr. Ettinger, Professor James L. Clifford, distinguished historian of Samuel Johnson and his circle, now deceased, proved to be particularly helpful through his reminiscences and his personal papers. I owe him my sincerest thanks.

In addition to the above, I was favored by correspondence and personal interviews with the three men who knew Ettinger best during his days at Brasenose: Leonard Hector, Donald Tyerman, and J. K. Creer. Most appropriately, Hector was interviewed at the old British Public Record Office on Chancery Lane, where he had spent his entire career and which had been Ettinger's Mecca; Tyerman I interviewed at his home in Buckingham Mansions, London; Creer and I met in a cozy public house hard by the British Museum. The insights these men possessed were very important in piecing the introduction together. If I have failed to recreate a bit of the life of Amos Aschbach Ettinger, then, it has been my fault and no one else's.

My thanks should also go to Miss Geraldine Le May and the staff at the Savannah Public Library, where I first viewed the Ettinger work that makes up the bulk of this volume. It had been while rummaging through several of the collections of the Georgia Historical Society that I first stumbled across a reference to its existence. The administrators and staff of the Georgia Historical Society in Hodgson Hall were, as ever, well informed and good humored. Lilla Mills Hawes was at that time director of the Society, and I am in her debt for the suggestion to publish the essay with an appropriate introduction. The staff at Oglethorpe University in Atlanta has also been helpful, and I was allowed free access to the Ettinger Collection in the University of Georgia's Rare Books and Manuscripts Division.

My appreciation also is extended to Oxford University and the elements there who oversee the various Beit interests. Although neither the university nor the Beit trustees have a proprietary right to past essays such as Ettinger's, they were uniformly cooperative and interested in seeing this publication come to fruition.

Over and above all, I am indebted to Kathryn Gable Ettinger who, as widow of the historian, has given me permission to publish this work. Mrs. Ettinger, "Kitty," has been exceedingly generous with her time and her recollections. She has led me to sources that I might otherwise have missed and has been consistently patient with a project that has now stretched over a full decade. I only hope that the end product is something of which she, her son, and her grandchildren can be proud.

I owe Professor Jack R. Pole of St. Catherine's College, Oxford, a special note of thanks for helping resolve with the university and Beit authorities the problems of the publication of the following essay. I also owe a hearty vote of thanks to Mrs. Jennie P. Johnson, patient proofer and drill master of the Index. And, as ever, my wife Margie who has a unique capacity to winnow the wheat from the chaff.

Phinizy Spalding

Preface

In his brilliant survey of English History, George Macaulay Tre-velyan has interpreted the eighteenth century as the age of the individ-ual. Acknowledging that its corporate institutions were "half asleep", he asserts that "the glory of the Eighteenth Century in Britain lay in the genius and energy of individuals acting freely in a free community."[1]

Ipso facto, the career of James Edward Oglethorpe stands forth as worthy of delineating in the approaching bi-centenary of his first great humanitarian endeavour. An outstanding figure of his age whom Doyle rightly calls "the founder of modern philanthropy",[2] and whom Austin Dobson so happily dubbed "a paladin of philanthropy",[3] Oglethorpe re-mains today a subject deserving of a modern Boswell as in his later years he was esteemed by Doctor Johnson and his famous biographer.[4]

Modern biography, giving ear to the siren song of the psycholo-gists, has placed increasing emphasis upon the heredity and environ-ment of the subject, a phase of analysis which, in Oglethorpe's career, demands marked consideration. Again, his "strong benevolence of

---

[1]Trevelyan, G. M. "History of England". London. 1926. p. 506.

[2]Doyle, J. A. "The English in America. The Colonies under the House of Han-over". London. 1907. p. 418.

[3]Dobson, Austin. "A Paladin of Philanthropy". London. 1899.

[4]Boswell, James. "Life of Samuel Johnson". Croker edition. 1867. p. 221. April 10, 1775.

soul", as Pope defined it,[5] must be noted in his humanitarian champi-
onship of reform of both debtor laws and penal institutions, and what
was a close ally thereof, his spiritual force as a leader in the broad tol-
erance of sundry sects. Attention must be given in the third place to his
views on vital political issues, national and international; nor may his
status in England be overlooked, for he was a colleague—aye, a
friend,—of Samuel Johnson, of Horace Walpole, of Boswell, Goldsmith, Burke, Pope and Hannah More; in short, of most of the social
and literary lights of the scintillant eighteenth century. Great however
as his career otherwise was, that phase which has attained paramount
importance and significance in history, was his activity in the foundation, propagation and preservation of an English colony in the New
World, wherein he united his philanthropic, spiritual and social forces
with a keen political philosophy, brilliant military strategy, and a practical sense of administration, to create for himself an abiding memorial
in the history of the British Empire.

Amos Aschbach Ettinger

---

[5]Pope, Alexander. "Imitations of Horace".Gilfillan edition. 1856. Two volumes.
Volume I, p. 273. Second Book, Second epistle, lines 276-277.

I

James Oglethorpe came of a family whose history would accord strictly with the psychological canons of heredity and environment. From his ancestors he derived three outstanding attributes: An abiding loyalty to the Crown; his military profession; and the parliamentary tradition.

Tracing a lineal descent from Ligulfe Theane of Oglethorpe in St. Edward the Confessor's reign,[1] an Oglethorpe maintained, at the cost of his life, the forlorn hope of the Anglo-Saxons against the Norman invaders. After centuries of residence on their Yorkshire estate, the military tradition of fealty was again manifested in the Civil Wars of the seventeenth century wherein the Oglethorpes suffered heavily in defense of the Crown, several of that name dying "in defense of Monarchy, in a battle near Oxford."[2] Sutton Oglethorpe, as they say, "for his loyalty to King Charles I was fined by the Parliament in the sum of 20,000*l.* for which his Estates were sequestered and afterwards forfeited."[3]

Sutton's son, Theophilus, was the first of the line to embody all three attributes. During the two decades succeeding the Restoration, he rose from the ranks of Charles II's lifeguards to a lieutenant-colonelcy

---

[1]The King's Collection of Stuart MSS., Windsor Castle. Fanny Oglethorpe to The Duke of Mar. December 23, 1717. By kind permission of His Majesty's Recorder of Archives. See also Manning and Bray. "History of Surrey", Volume I, p. 637.

[2]Nichols, John, editor. "Literary Anecdotes of the Eighteenth Century". Nine volumes. London. 1812-1815. Volume II, p. 17.

[3]Manning and Bray. "History of Surrey". Volume I, p. 610.

of dragoons. In accordance with prevalent social and military customs, he bartered appointments, fought and won duels, and, although his tactics have been severely criticized by a modern authority,[4] achieved a knighthood from his king and honourable mention by Macaulay[5] in defense of the Crown during Monmouth's rebellion. But his loyalty to James II cost him not only his regiment,[6] but also his profession for the "Glorious Revolution" was to him a debacle. Refusing to serve against his king, he retired to the Manor of Westbrook in Godalming, Surrey. Here with his wife, Eleanor Wall, a famous Irish beauty, whose father had also lost his estate in the revolution;[7] who was related to the House of Argyle; and who, moreover, was a confidante of the exiled monarch; here he remained until, branded as a Jacobite, he fled to France where, at the pseudo-court of James II he acclaimed his wife's efforts in the lost cause. Returning to England in 1694 they continued their machinations until 1698 when Sir Theophilus finally took the oath of allegiance to King William, and was immediately elected to represent Haslemere in Parliament. The parliamentary tradition was continued by his re-election in 1700 and the succession of his sons, Lewis in 1702 to his death in 1704, and Theophilus from 1708 to 1713.[8]

If it be that James Oglethorpe inherited the military zeal and parliamentary tradition from his father, then is it likewise true that he owed an equal share of his intense loyalty to the Crown, together with his staunch moral courage and high purpose, to his mother. The removal of the family to London, upon the election of Sir Theophilus to Parlia-

---

[4]Wolseley, General Viscount, K.P. "The Life of John Churchill, Duke of Marlborough, to the Accession of Queen Anne". Two volumes. London. 1894. Volume I, p. 324.

[5]Macaulay, T. B. "History of England". Tenth edition. Five volumes. London. 1854-1861. Volume I, pp. 593-594. See also Taylor, F. "The Wars of Marlborough, 1702-1709". Two volumes. Oxford. 1921. Volume II, pp. 411-428, *passim*.

[6]Wolseley, *op. cit.* Volume I, p. 322.

[7]The King's Collection of Stuart MSS. Fanny Oglethorpe to the Duke of Mar. December 23, 1717. By courtesy of His Majesty's Recorder of Archives, Windsor.

[8]The various details in the lives of Sir Theophilus and Lady Oglethorpe have been assembled from the numerous volumes of Reports of the Historical Manuscripts Commission.

ment in 1698, gave Lady Oglethorpe such ample scope for the exercise of her political propensities that from the Jacobite movement of 1690 to her death in 1732 she maintained the old doctrines with unswerving loyalty. She, far more than her husband, was a guiding spirit in the Jacobite movement and her defense thereof utterly disgusted her friend, Dean Swift, in whose eyes she was "so cunning a devil".[9] Such, then, was the heritage of James Oglethorpe.

[9]Scott, Temple, editor. "The Prose Works of Jonathan Swift". Twelve volumes. Volume II. "The Journal to Stella". p. 299.

II

James Edward Oglethorpe was born in London on December 22, 1696, and was baptized the following day at St. Martin's-in-the-Fields.[1] Every account to date of his first twenty years has been largely an essay in controversy, beginning with his birth, which for many years was held to be June 1, 1689, the birthday of a James Oglethorpe, son of Theophilus and Eleanor Wall Oglethorpe, duly recorded in St. James' Parish, London. This was an elder brother who either died in infancy, or as Mrs. Shaftoe's much-maligned narrative asserts, was substituted for the Old Pretender. The latter view, long scouted, has attained some credence by the evidence in the Harley letters of Mrs. Shaftoe's connexions with the Oglethorpe family, and their subsequent close alliance with the Jacobite court in France.[2]

---

[1]"Notes and Queries". Third series. Volume X. 1867. p. 63; Georgia Historical Society Collections. Volume VII, Part II, pp. 12, 41-51. The year is proved correct by Rawlinson MSS. (Letters), 92. f. 602. Bodleian Library. In January, 1714, James Edward Oglethorpe, born in December, 1696, was in "the seventeenth year of his age."

[2]Shaftoe, Frances. "An Account of Her being Eleven Months in Sir Theophilus Oglethorpe's Family", etc. First edition. London. 1707; second edition. London. 1745. Also "More Memoirs: or, the Pretender What He Really Pretends to be", etc. London. 1713. The evidence herein found coincides remarkably with material found in the Hist. MSS. Com. Reports. Volume 29. Fifteenth Report. Appendix, Part IV. Portland MSS. Volume IV. Harley Letters and Papers. Volume II, pp. 284, 317, 377, 402 and 417. Also Volume IX, p. 220. Hannah More in 1784 speaks of James Edward Oglethorpe as a "foster-brother to the Pretender". Roberts, Wm. "Memoirs of the Life of Mrs. Hannah More". Two volumes. London. 1836. p. 256.

While James Edward's early years are veiled in mystery, he has recorded in a letter written in his retirement, the impressions he gained from seeing, in the days of his youth, the great men of the age: "Even from my childhood I made it my business to see all the great men of my time from Lewis the 14th and Victor Amadeus, two kings, and the truly great Prince Eugene down to the poor spirited, coviteous Duke of Marlborough, and good King John of Portugal."[3]

His mother's activities remain the sole indication of the training he received, for his later youth was inextricably interwoven with her Jacobite career. Having sought political preferment for her elder son, Theophilus,[4] and matrimonial position with a title in France for her daughter, Eleanor,[5] she now used her influence upon Marlborough for her "Jamie".

In his study of English Army Lists, Dalton asserts that before 1709 James Oglethorpe obtained a commission from Marlborough as Ensign in the 1st Foot Guards which, however, was not officially forthcoming.[6] In 1712 he is recorded to have offered five horses for the campaign in Flanders,[7] and on November 21 of the next year he was commissioned at Windsor to be Lieutenant unassigned and rank as Captain of Foot.[8] But the military life gave way temporarily at least to the academic.

At an indeterminate date about this time the youth, following the precedent of his elder brothers who had been there in 1698,[9] entered

---

[3]Hist. MSS. Com. Volume 8. Ninth Report. Lord Elphinstone Collection, p. 229a. Letter of Oglethorpe to Field-Marshal Keith. Rotterdam. May 3, 1756.

[4]*Ibid.* Volume 29. Fifteenth Report. Appendix. Part IV. Portland MSS. Volume IV. Harley Letters and Papers. Volume II. Lady Oglethorpe to Robert Harley. September 6, 1710, p. 590; September 24, 1710, p. 600; Theophilus Oglethorpe to Robert Harley, October 8, 1710, p. 610.

[5]"Gentleman's Magazine". Volume LV. 1785. Part II, p. 602.

[6]Dalton, Charles. "English Army Lists, and Commission Registers, 1661-1714". Volume VI, p. 53.

[7]*Ibid.*, p. 391.

[8]*Ibid.*, p. 51.

[9]Austen-Leigh, R.A. "Eton College Lists, 1678-1790". p. 258.

Eton College.[10] Here he remained while his mother continued her Jacobite machinations. Despite a warning from Marlborough that he and she were suspected of a plot against the court,[11] she steadfastly pursued her policy. Thus, early in 1714 she determined to place her Eton son under proper Jacobite influences at Corpus Christi College, Oxford. She therefore sought the aid of her ally, the non-juring bishop, George Hickes, who on January 12, 1714, wrote thus to Dr. Thomas Turner, President of the college and brother of the Jacobite Bishop Turner: "Yesterday my Lady Ogilthorp did me the favour to give me a visit as to her son yet a scholar at Eaton-school. He is a very ingenious, understanding, and well-bred youth in the 17th year of his age. I found by her Lad(yshi)ps discourses at last, that the chief end of her visit was to let you know by me how desirous she was to have him, as his eldest brother formerly was, a fellow commoner of your College, under your inspection. She makes it her earnest request to you y^t (that) you would keep a place void for him and saith (that) she had written for that purpose to Mr. Perrot, but seemed troubled (that) she had no answer for him, and therefore I pray you to send an answer to her by him, or me, or immediately to herself, if you are acquainted with her. . . ."[12]

The plea was successful and he entered Corpus Christi College on July 3, 1714,[13] matriculating in the University five days later.[14] As President Fowler has written, "Oglethorpe's is an early instance, probably the first in Corpus in the case of a non-foundationer, of 'keeping the name on the books' during a prolonged period of non-residence. His name first disappears on May 3, 1717; it was re-entered on June 25,

---

[10]Rawlinson MSS. J. 4°. VI. 34. Bodleian Library.

[11]Hist. MSS. Com. Volume 7. Eighth Report. Appendix. Part I. Marlborough Papers, p. 14a. Marlborough to Lady Oglethorpe. London. July 4, 1713.

[12]Rawlinson MSS. (Letters). 92. f. 609. Bodleian Library. This letter with its reference to Oglethorpe "in the 17th year of his age" early in 1714, proves his birth year.

[13]Fowler, Thomas. "The History of Corpus Christi College, with Lists of its Members", p. 275.

[14]Foster, Joseph. "Alumni Oxonienses". Early Series, 1500-1714. Four volumes. Volume III, p. 1086.

1719, and finally disappears on October 20, 1727."[15] This accords well
with his economic status for the re-entry on the books follows within a
year his succession to Westbrook and the family fortune. "For the
greater part of the time after re-entering his name he does not battel,"
wrote Fowler,[16] and "he seems never to have proceeded to the Degree of
B.A., but when he had for some years been Member for Haslemere,
and had already obtained considerable reputation for his philanthropic
efforts on behalf of imprisoned debtors, he was specially created M.A.
on July 31, 1731."[17] His interest in Corpus Christi College never waned
and in 1772 he presented to it what is now a cherished memento, two
beautifully illuminated volumes of the French History of the Bible.

Although he kept his name on the books of the College, Oglethorpe remained but a short time in residence. His army commission
was renewed in 1715 by George I who assigned him to the first troop of
the Queen's Guards, but the "Wanderlust" had seized him and, prefer-
ring possible action abroad to inertia at home, he resigned from the
army in 1716.[18] As his sisters were already in France, he now migrated
to Paris, where at the Academy he became a fellow-student with the future Field-Marshal Keith.[19] But the desire for action was always strong
within him and the campaign of Prince Eugene of Savoy against the
Turks gave him his opportunity. Early in 1717 he eluded the French em-
bargo on foreign service[20] and joined the Prince's circle as his aide-de-
camp. Here, as Boswell relates it, he received his first lesson in diplomacy in an encounter at the table with a Prince of Wurtemburg. The
latter, having cleverly fillipped some wine from his glass into Ogle-

---

[15]Fowler, *op. cit.*, p. 275.

[16]*Ibid.*, p. 440.

[17]*Ibid.*, p. 279.

[18]Dalton, *op. cit.* Volume VI, p. 53.

[19]Hist. MSS. Com. Volume 8. Ninth Report. Lord Elphinstone Collection, p.
229a. Letter of Oglethorpe to Field-Marshal Keith. December 9, 1755. For proof of
Keith's presence at the Academy, see article on Keith in the Dictionary of National Biography. 1921 reprint. Oxford. Volume X, p. 1212.

[20]Hist. MSS. Com. Volume 56. The King's Collection of Stuart MSS. Volume
IV, p. 171. The Duke of Mar. to James III (Paris). April 8, 1717.

thorpe's face, the youth with a disarming and engaging smile exclaimed: "That's a good joke, but we do it much better in England", at that moment flinging an entire glassful of wine into the astonished royal countenance, to the great amusement and admiration of the company.[21] In this environment he spent the next year and by his military capabilities achieved merited distinction and the approval of his superiors. To the great pride of his sisters, he mounted the trenches in the famous battle of Belgrade on August 3, 1717,[22] which he described to his sister Fanny as "very bloody and sharp", and wherein he was unharmed although "his servant that was next to him is killed."[23] With this Austrian victory, his account of which was to fascinate Doctor Johnson over fifty years later,[24] the war soon came to a close, leaving Oglethorpe with a high and deserved military reputation, remarkable for a youth of twenty-two.

Although he had been reared on Jacobite doctrine, his continental army career might have nullified the effect thereof, had not his family again taken him in hand. The failure of the Jacobite movement of 1710 and the death in 1714 of Queen Anne, last of the Stuarts, had driven the Oglethorpes to the quasi-court of James III at Saint Germain. Here Anne and Fanny, the two unmarried sisters, basking the while in the royal favour, plotted assiduously with the aid of Eleanor, now Mme. de Mezières, for the eventual return of the exile. The accession of George I led to a great counter-movement of Jacobites in France, including an invasion of Scotland, in which Anne and Fanny became liaison officers, so to speak, between the court at Saint Germain and the conspirators at home, chief among whom were Lady Eleanor Wall Oglethorpe, as ardent as ever, and her fourth daughter, Molly. Theophilus, now head of the family, having been defeated for re-election to Parliament, left England in the Earl of Peterborough's retinue in 1714, never to return, and eventually became the Jacobite representative at the court of the King of Sicily in Turin. The Stuart Papers at Windsor reveal most interestingly

---

[21]Boswell, *op. cit.*, pp. 173-174. April 10, 1772.

[22]Hist. MSS. Com. Volume 56. The King's Collection of Stuart MSS. Volume IV, p. 534. Fanny Oglethorpe to the Duke of Mar. Paris. August 27, 1717.

[23]*Ibid.*, pp. 539-540. Fanny Oglethorpe to Mar. August 28, 1717.

[24]Boswell, *op. cit.*, p. 174. April 10, 1772.

the machinations of these workers in the "lost cause" between 1715 and 1720, and the evidences of blind, unwavering loyalty on the part of the Oglethorpes often border on the pathetic.[25] Toward the end of 1717 the sisters conceived the idea that their joint family labours deserved regal recognition. Basing their claims in general on centuries of family loyalty to the Crown, and in particular on James II's desire at Bothwell Bridge to make Colonel Theophilus Oglethorpe a baronet, which as Fanny Oglethorpe charged, jealous rivals had prevented,[26] they now asked James III to confer some distinction preferably a baronetcy, upon Theophilus, with remainder to James Oglethorpe who for this purpose was regarded as his brother's son.[27] This the Pretender did on December 20, creating Theophilus Baron Oglethorpe of Oglethorpe, with remainders to his direct heirs or brother, James. James Oglethorpe was therefore an embryonic recipient of the only Jacobite peerage of this period other than the Earldom given to the Duke of Mar, James III's loyal aide.[28] This of itself indicates the position of the Oglethorpe connexion in Jacobite history and goes far toward substantiating the Shaftoe narrative.

With the close of the campaign against the Turks James Oglethorpe returned to his sisters in Paris by way of Turin, Italy, where, through his brother, Mar had met him.[29] The Jacobites now saw a use for "Jamie", concerning whom his sister, Fanny, wrote that "truth is that he is a very good youth and has a true foundation of honest principles." As he was shortly to leave for England to settle his brother's domestic

---

[25]Hist. MSS. Com. Volume 56. The King's Collection of Stuart MSS. Volumes II-VIII. *Passim*. For Volume VIII in MSS. at the Public Record Office, I am indebted to His Majesty's Recorder of Archives at Windsor, and S. C. Ratcliff Esq., of the Historical Manuscripts Commission.

[26]The King's Collection of Stuart MSS. at Windsor. Fanny Oglethorpe to Mar. December 23, 1717. Unpublished letter, quoted by the king permission of His Majesty's Recorder of Archives. Written after James III had approved the request.

[27]Hist. MSS. Com. Volume 56. Stuart MSS. Volume V, pp. 229-232. Fanny Oglethorpe to Mar. November 24, 1717.

[28]*Ibid*. pp. xxvii-xxviii and 289. James III to his Attorney or Solicitor-General of England, Urbino. December 20, 1717.

[29]*Ibid*., p. 232. Fanny Oglethorpe to Mar. November 24, 1717.

affairs, the idea was conceived of making him a Stuart messenger.[30] In December, 1717, however, he decided to go to Rome where his brother then was. The Jacobite stamp was rapidly yet thoroughly being applied. "He intends," wrote Fanny to Mar, who was then with James III at Urbino, Italy, "to ask to kiss our Master's hand. I suppose he'll address himself to you. He is charmed with your goodness to him at T[urin]."[31] Mar had often asked about "Jamie",[32] which highly pleased Theophilus, who, waiting in Rome until his brother's arrival in January, 1718,[33] added his own approval to that of Fanny: "I am very well satisfied with him and love him the more, because I see he is entirely affectionate to the King and that the Germans have not in the least prevailed on him."[34] By February 12 Theophilus could write: "My brother is gone hence to pay his duty to his Majesty, being pushed by the natural zeal that belongs to the family."[35] Returning from court, where, as Mar wrote, the royal exile "was well pleased with [him], and I believe James no less with him",[36] James Oglethorpe paused in Rome to send Mar his thanks for the civilities received at his hands, and to assure him how sensible he was and always would be of the king's great goodness to him.[37] By this time the lad was strongly and surely identified with the cause. Theophilus now turned toward Naples where he almost fell into the clutches of the British Navy, but escaped to Malta,[38] while James rejoined his

---

[30]Hist. MSS. Com. Volume 56. Stuart MSS. Volume V, p. 231. Fanny Oglethorpe to Mar. November 24, 1717.

[31]Ibid. p. 276. Fanny Oglethorpe to Mar. December 14, 1717.

[32]Ibid. p. 284. Mar to Fanny Oglethorpe. Urbino, Italy. December 16, 1717.

[33]Ibid. p. 351. Theophilus Oglethorpe to Mar. Rome. January 1, 1718; p. 383. Same to same. Rome. January 12, 1718; p. 466. Mar to Anne Oglethorpe. February 12, 1718.

[34]Ibid. p. 401. Theophilus Oglethorpe to Mar. Rome. January 22, 1718.

[35]Hist. MSS. Com. Volume 56. Stuart MSS. Volume V, p. 459. Theophilus Oglethorpe to Mar. Rome. February 12, 1718.

[36]Ibid. p. 494. Mar to Fanny Oglethorpe. Urbino. February 19, 1718. See also Volume VI, p. 138. Mar to Anne Oglethorpe. Urbino. March 11, 1718.

[37]Ibid. Volume V, p. 512. James Oglethorpe to Mar. Rome. February 26, 1718.

[38]Ibid. Volume VII, p. 198. Theophilus Oglethorpe to Mar. Malta. August 24, 1718.

sisters in France preparatory to the long-delayed return to England. Anne Oglethorpe having asked the king to accept her thanks for "your particular marks of favour to my brother, James, till God enables him to acknowledge them by his services,"[39] her sisters proposed to Mar that, as James was soon returning to England, he would "execute any orders you may have for him with the zeal and attachment which he and the rest of the family have for all orders coming from the master and you."[40] So it was that in September, 1718, Fanny could write to Mar that "Jimmy is here and going home, very sensible of the goodness *the King* had for him, which he'll never forget."[41] The inoculation of Jacobite virus was presumably a success.

Although the lad had succumbed in the Jacobite atmosphere of France and Italy, there appeared, however, no guarantee that, away from those influences, he would remain true to the cause. With the year 1719 the Oglethorpe influence at Saint Germain perceptibly declined and it is therefore not strange that henceforth no mention is made of the youth in the Stuart manuscripts.[42]

In his volume on "The English in America", J. A. Doyle has asserted that, while Theophilus and Anne Oglethorpe had "drifted farther into Jacobitism than their father, . . . the support given by James Oglethorpe to the fallen cause was of a soberer type, and after the Hanoverian accession he enlisted himself among the followers of Windham. The outward conduct and policy of Oglethorpe reflected the more rational and reputable side of Jacobitism."[43] This statement is true only in its summation. The new evidence, above presented, indicates the strength of the Jacobite influence to which the youth was exposed in his formative years as well as the spread among *all* the Oglethorpes of the Jacobite

---

[39]*Ibid*. Volume VI, p. 260. Anne Oglethorpe to James III. March 25-April 5, 1718.

[40]Hist. MSS. Com. Volume 56. Stuart MSS. Volume VII, p. 215. Madame de Mezières to Mar. Paris. August 29, 1718. See also pp. 157-158. Fanny Oglethorpe to Mar. From France. August 15, 1718.

[41]*Ibid*., p. 299. Fanny Oglethorpe to Mar. September 19, 1718.

[42]*Ibid*., Volume VIII. *Passim*. MSS. at the Public Record Office, examined by courtesy of His Majesty's Recorder of Archives at Windsor, and S. C. Ratcliff Esq.

[43]Doyle, *op. cit.*, p. 416.

"drift", and stamps as all the more remarkable the later "rational" attitude of James Oglethorpe in the Hanoverian era.

The young veteran now returned to England where he shortly succeeded his errant brother as incumbent of the family estate at Westbrook. Despite the seemingly auspicious inoculation, he took no part in the ebb and flow of Jacobite fortune. Here he seems to have remained for the next three years in innocuous desuetude until in 1722 he emerged from his rural retreat to become a candidate for Parliament.

III

In the early spring of 1722 James Oglethorpe was elected to represent the borough of Haslemere in the House of Commons. For the next thirty-two years his name stood upon the list of members but not without strong opposition. His parliamentary activities, hitherto somewhat overshadowed in history by his subsequent career, fall into three categories: his struggles for re-election; his famed efforts on behalf of imprisoned debtors; and his less widely known, but equally important, views on problems of vital national or imperial import.

From his first candidacy, he faced the virulent opposition of the Whig oligarchy. There lies among the manuscripts of the Marquess Townshend, at that time Secretary of State, a list of election returns up to March 28, 1722, wherein James Oglethorpe and Peter Burrell were voted as opposition members for Haslemere. This return was declared to be false by the Ministry who claimed Lord Blundell and Mr. Molineux, their candidates, to have been duly chosen, but, as the election does not seem to have been challenged, Oglethorpe and Burrell took their seats in the House, where they remained unchallenged until 1734.[1]

Taking his seat on October 9, 1722, Oglethorpe became under Wyndham an Hanoverian Tory colleague of the great leaders of the Whig ascendancy.[2] As Mr. Keith Feiling has shown in his "History of

---

[1]Hist. MSS. Com. Volume 19. Eleventh Report. Appendix. Part IV. MSS. of the Marquess Townshend, pp. 136-137.

[2]Hervey, John, Lord, "Memoirs of the Reign of George the Second". J. W. Croker, editor. Two volumes. London. 1848. Volume I. Chapter I, pp. 1-29.

the Tory Party", the Revolution of 1688 had effected the decline of the
Tories due to their Jacobite adhesion, with the result that after the first
parliament of Queen Anne in 1702 and still more upon the ministerial
revolution of 1710, the Whigs had attained an impregnable ascendancy
which not even a party scandal could destroy.[3] The leadership of Robert
Walpole, as John Morley has pointed out, rose above the South Sea Bub-
ble; discomfited the Jacobites who, encouraged by the popular discontent, engendered by that affair, had planned a Stuart restoration; and
created the great imperial movements of the eighteenth century.[4]

In such an atmosphere Oglethorpe, Tory son and brother of Jacobite loyalists, took no part in debate until April 6, 1723, when, by a
queer turn of fate, the Commons were debating the punishment to be
meted out to Dr. Francis Atterbury, Bishop of Rochester, who was ac-
cused of complicity in a Catholic plot for the restoration of "the Popish
Pretender", James III. Exhibiting most markedly in this, his maiden
effort, the "soberer type" of support for the Jacobite cause, the new
member for Haslemere opposed the proposed banishment of the bishop.
Deprecating the powers of the Pretender whom, a bare five years before, he had well-nigh worshipped, but who now, he declared, "it was
plain . . . had none but a company of silly fellows about him," Oglethorpe opposed the punishment of Atterbury on the grounds of expe-
diency, fearing that, "if the bishop, who was allowed to be a man of great
parts, should be banished, he might be solicited and tempted to go to
Rome, and there be in a capacity to do more mischief by his advice, than
if he was suffered to stay in England under the watchful eye of those in
power."[5] His appeal, however, failed, the measure was approved, and
with it no more is heard of Oglethorpe in Parliament until the inquiry
"into the State of the Gaols of the Kingdom" early in 1729.

The inquiry which was to bring Oglethorpe into prominence was
the result of the state of the times. The England of Oglethorpe's earlier
years still retained the Restoration viewpoint on morals. As Lecky de-

---

[3]Feiling, Keith G. "A History of the Tory Party, 1640-1714". Oxford. 1924. *Passim*, especially pp. 480-481.

[4]Morley, John. "Walpole". Twelve English Statesmen. London. 1922. Chapters
III and IV. *Passim*.

[5]"Cobbett's Parliamentary History of England". Volume VIII, p. 216.

clared, "of the active reforming and philanthropic spirit which became so conspicuous in the reign of George III we find scarcely any traces."[6] One of the worst problems of the period was the legal status of debtors. Holdsworth has shown, in his "History of the English Law", how the early systems of law made the obligation of the debtor personal in such an extremely literal sense that the body of the debtor could be taken by the creditor. Modes of legal procedure gradually changed but this provision was a vital source of relief and survived throughout the years. As a result of this policy, asserts Holdsworth, "constraint of the debtor's person thus became in England a more general method of execution than in many other countries in Europe" and "was entirely unregulated. The results can be read in the pages of Dickens." A demand arising for relief by legislation, numerous acts were passed in the latter part of the seventeenth century, but "the number of these Acts leads us to think that they were not very effectual, either to procure the release of prisoners, or to put a stop to the malpractices of gaolers or their officers" who, indeed, "were more likely to side with rich creditors then poor debtors."[7]

This system of sanctioning the incarceration of an individual, often in a foul dungeon, and solely at the behest of his creditors, led to the imprisonment of a man named Castell who, unable to pay the fees with which gaolers mulcted their unfortunate charges, was confined in a house where prevailed small-pox, from which he subsequently died. He had been a friend of Oglethorpe who, but for this event, so Lecky asserts, "would probably have remained an undistinguished Member of Parliament." Be that as it may, "this incident directed the attention of Oglethorpe to the management of the prisons."[8] Convinced that his friend's death was due to existent penal conditions, he began a movement for reform. Pressing for an investigation he succeeded in obtaining, on February 25, 1729, the appointment by the Commons of a committee of fourteen with himself as chairman to institute a parliamentary inquiry into "the State of the Gaols of this Kingdom." The inquiry, which

---

[6]Lecky, W. E. H. "A History of England in the Eighteenth Century". Eight volumes. London. 1878. Volume I, pp. 498-499.

[7]Holdsworth, W. S. "A History of English Law". Third edition. Nine volumes. London. 1922. Volume VIII, pp. 229-245, *passim*.

[8]Lecky, *op. cit.* Volume I, p. 500.

began with the Fleet Prison, a relic of the Court of Star Chamber, led the committee to examine numerous imprisoned debtors who, for their testimony prejudicial to their respective wardens, were often cast into chains. The committee was so zealous that the judges and other officials thus exposed began to vilify its members. Although Oglethorpe informed a colleague that "I was not very willing to revive the Committee, because I knew the ill will the Administration bore it; and the weight of the judges and Court would be against us," it was nevertheless renewed on February 21, 1730, because it "was necessary for our reputations, being vilified for proceeding so zealously last year."[9] They therefore continued their investigations which now embraced the Prison of the Court of Marshalsea; the King's Palace Court of Westminster, and the King's Bench Prison. As Tindal has well said, "the farther the Committee proceeded in their enquiries, the more dismal and shocking was the scene of cruelty, barbarity and extortion which they disclosed."[10]

As a result of these investigations Oglethorpe presented three reports to the Commons in which he charged the respective wardens and their deputies with the sale of offices, breaches of trust, great extortions, and the highest crimes and misdemeanours. In his last report, after citing a long succession of evils, he uttered this dire prophecy: "If this be law, all England may be made one extended prison." Largely as a result of his impassioned zeal, the House accepted the proposals for the reform of the prison system, and for preventing the "Judges, their clerks and servants, from receiving any Fees, Gifts, Presents, or any gratuities whatsoever."[11] Oglethorpe had done his work thoroughly in compiling and presenting the reports. As Henry Bruce has so aptly phrased it, "these reports lie before me now, in sixty or seventy of the dim and stained pages of Cobbett's old Parliamentary History. They are not exhilarating reading. Here are a score of cases as bad as Castell's; here are

---

[9]Hist. MSS. Com. Volume 63. "Diary of the Earl of Egmont". (Hereinafter cited as "Egmont Diary"). Three volumes. Volume I, p. 46. February 13, 1730; p. 50. February 17; p. 55, February 21, 1730.

[10]"Tindal's Continuation of Rapin's History of England". Cited in "Cobbett's Parliamentary History of England". Volume VIII, p. 707 note.

[11]"Cobbett's Parliamentary History of England". Volume VIII, pp. 706-731; 731-753; 803-826.

some cases much worse. The yellow pages, like the leaves in Dante's do-
lorous wood, seem to cry out with strong agony as one touches them";[12]
and Wright has justly affirmed of them that therein "those who delight
in sensational reading will—if facts can yield them as much pleasure as
fiction—find much thrilling matter."[13]

Action now rested with the government, which proceeded to state
trials of the principal miscreants. The reports of these trials are far from
edifying reading and the result, a general acquittal of the defendants on
all charges, nullifies to a great extent the value of reading the time-worn
pages: as one edition of Howell asserts, "it is remarkable that, though
the prosecutions against Mr. Huggins, Mr. Bambridge, etc., were ordered by his Majesty, on an Address from the House of Commons, and
conducted by some of the greatest men at the bar, yet they got off—all
being acquitted."[14] After the trials commenced, Oglethorpe spoke but
once; yet here again he manifested his strong sense of justice and obe-
dience to the spirit, as well as the letter, of the law. William Acton, Deputy Keeper of Marshalsea Prison, had been acquitted on a charge of
murder. He therefore asked for his discharge, a plea which the crown
attorney refused to support. Acton's lawyer then asked Oglethorpe, who
had attended all the trials, to consent to a discharge. In noble phrases the
latter explained that, as he was not the person to decide this, he refused
to do so but, he continued, "were I prosecutor, I should desire the pris-
oner might be released; not that I think him innocent, but that every
Englishman, let him be never so unjustly acquitted, hath, by the Ha-
beas Corpus Act, on his acquittal, a right to be discharged."[15]

The decisions were thus eminently unsatisfactory, but the worst
abuses of the *ancien régime* were exterminated and England was the better for Oglethorpe's labours which, declares Wright, although "too
soon forgotten, were universally applauded at the time."[16] Chief among

---

[12]Bruce, Henry. "Life of General Oglethorpe". New York. 1890. p. 47.

[13]Wright, Robert. "Life of General James Edward Oglethorpe". London. 1867.
p. 29.

[14]Howell, T. B. "A Complete Collection of State Trials". London. 1813. Volume
XVII, p. 616.

[15]*Ibid.*, pp. 502-503.

[16]Wright, *op. cit.*, p. 23.

these contemporary tributes was that of James Thomson, the poet, who, in his study of the "Seasons", lauded with joy

> "the glorious band
> Who, touched with human woe, redressive searched
> Into the horrors of the gloomy jail."[17]

Even though the goal was not fully achieved, the episode was pregnant with consequences for Oglethorpe's future career.

The prominence of this particular question in the history of eighteenth century England has overshadowed Oglethorpe's part in debate upon other issues. No longer the parliamentary novice, tainted with Jacobite ancestry, he now evinced an interest in national affairs which, to almost as great a degree as the penal problem, were to influence his future career.

In the same session as that which authorized the prison investigations, Oglethorpe, whose objection to alcohol, in Austin Dobson's words, "stopped at 'firewater',"[18] expressed his approval of temperance by proposing a further duty on malt "as well to discourage the pernicious use of spirits, such as gin, etc, as encourage the drinking [of] malt liquors."[19] He attacked royal extravagance in opposing a grant of £115,000 to cover arrearages in the king's civil list.[20] He opposed the government on the question of English participation in settling the peace of Europe,[21] but the next year began his persistent advocacy of military preparedness. On a bill for further troops, Oglethorpe, notes Egmont, "on this occasion voted for the Court, though a very obstinate Tory, and gave for reason, that he believed we should go into a war with the Emperor, and therefore thought it necessary to have an army", especially, as he put it, "while things stand as they do in Europe." As to the army's

---

[17]Thomson, James. "Seasons". Gilfillan edition. 1853. "Winter". Volume I, p. 144. lines 359-362 ff.

[18]Dobson, *op. cit.*, p. 14 note.

[19]"Egmont Diary". Volume III. Appendix, p. 344. February, 1729.

[20]"Cobbett's Parliamentary History of England". Volume VIII, p. 706.

[21]"Egmont Diary". Volume III. Appendix, p. 345.

nationality, "he had rather see an army of Englishmen than foreigners among us." He preferred, moreover, that English and Irish troops be sent to the Continent in lieu of Hessians, as they would behave as well as the Germans, would thus gain experience, and would serve to introduce English goods on the continent, which would aid English trade.[22] At home he demanded reduction of the Sinking Fund "which he thought was grown so great that it might prove prejudicial to the kingdom's safety, and absolutely undo it if it fell in the hands of a bad Ministry";[23] and he proclaimed the right of petition at all times.[24]

In 1731 the European situation had caused him to reiterate his views on the army. Continuing his staunch advocacy of preparedness, he nevertheless strongly opposed the perennial hire of Hessian troops—a favourite Hanoverian practice—on the grounds that it entailed spending British money to uphold the Georgian dynasty in Germany.[25] His strong sense of right appeared in the debate on the Pension Bill which he favoured. In answering a member who, in attacking the measure, had spoken of "wicked and desperate opposition", Oglethorpe asserted that "none who speak for liberty can do it wickedly and desperately,"[26] declaring in the same speech that "men who discharge their consciences faithfully will be little solicitous of being again in Parliament."[27] In all this, although he opposed the administration, the member for Haslemere firmly proclaimed the legitimacy of the Hanoverian dynasty. In a debate wherein emphatic affirmative references had been made to parliamentary limitation of the king's authority, it was freely admitted that Oglethorpe, "who was never a Courtier, said that he *trembled to hear the King's Title thus drawn into the question*."[28]

---

[22]*Ibid.*, Volume I, pp. 12, 13 and 26. January 29-February 4, 1730.

[23]*Ibid.*, p. 63. February 25, 1730.

[24]*Ibid.*, p. 68.

[25]*Ibid.*, p. 126. February 3, 1731. Also Hist. MSS. Com. Volume 42. Fifteenth Report. Appendix. Part VI. "Manuscripts of the Earl of Carlisle", p. 81. Colonel the Honourable Charles Howard to Lord Carlisle. February 4, 1731.

[26]*Ibid.*, p. 134. February, 1731. See also "Carlisle MSS." p. 82. Howard to Carlisle. February 23, 1731.

[27]*Ibid.*, p. 140.

[28]"Gentleman's Magazine". Volume I. 1731. p. 278.

With the opening of Parliament in January, 1732, there arose an international complication. England had become involved in numerous treaties and conventions with continental powers for whom she spent money often without just cause or adequate protection. Petitions now came in from seaport merchants complaining of Spanish depredations upon their West Indian commerce. At the same time the king in his speech from the throne proclaimed the general tranquillity of Europe and the confirmation of the Pragmatic Sanction in the Treaty of Vienna. It was quite manifest that Walpole was attempting to quell discontent at home and cover administration blunders by directing attention to his continental diplomacy. Much as he disliked opposing the reply to the king "for our Kings ought to be respected, and if we dislike anything, it is the Ministry we must level our resentment at,"[29] Oglethorpe felt compelled to withhold his approval of a reply which embodied expressions implying blind acquiescence in every ministerial measure. He now renewed his attacks on the disarmament policy of the administration, demanding "full and complete satisfaction for the many depredations committed by the Spaniards," and expressing a desire "to see more care taken in arming the country and disciplining our militia." Thus staunchly advocating preparedness, he doubted the immediate importance of the Pragmatic Sanction as compared with "many other things which at present relate more nearly to the honour and interest of this nation," chief of which was naturally the national defence.[30] Turning to foreign affairs he publicly manifested for the first time his interest in the oppressed Protestants of Salzburg in Germany. These, as Strobel narrates in his history of the sect, were Lutherans, now immortalized in Goethe's "Hermann und Dorothea", who were driven hither and thither in Central Europe by the continued persecutions of Archbishop Leopold of Salzburg, persecutions which ultimately led thirty thousand of them to seek safety in England and Holland.[31] Their plight, so well described by Carlyle,[32]

---

[29]"Egmont Diary". Volume I, p. 215. January 13, 1732.

[30]"Cobbett's Parliament History of England". Volume VIII, pp. 875-876.

[31]*Ibid.*, and Strobel, P. A. "The Salzburgers and their Descendants". Baltimore, Maryland. 1855. pp. 25-43, *passim.*

[32]Carlyle, Thomas. "Frederick the Great". Ten volumes. London. No date. Volume III. Chapter III, pp. 123-143.

now revived in Oglethorpe that humanitarian impulse which had been prominent in the late prison inquiry.

Oglethorpe had now placed himself on record as a mild High Tory, an opponent of royal extravagance and of Walpole's autocratic mismanagement in domestic affairs, a guiding spirit in the prison inquiries, a protagonist of national defense and anti-continental isolation, and an ardent advocate for the spiritually oppressed. He now exhibited no less an interest in the mercantile and imperial spheres of British policy. Late in January, 1732, a bill "for the better securing and encouraging the trade of his Majesty's Sugar Colonies in America" came before the House. In strict accordance with extant colonial policy of the mercantile system, this measure gave preference to the West Indian insular colonies by prohibiting commerce between the French islands and the colonies on the North American continent. This aroused the opposition of many members of the Commons, some from their personal interest in the continental colonies, others like Oglethorpe from their wider view of affairs. In phrases which presage the principles of Burke, of Franklin and of Jefferson, and proclaim at once the unity of the Empire and the equality of all its citizens, wherever situate, Oglethorpe now expounded the doctrine that "in all cases that come before this House, where there seems to be a clashing of interests between one set of people and another, we ought to have no regard to the particular interest of any country or set of people; the good of the whole is what we ought only to have under our consideration: our colonies are all a part of our own dominions; the people in every one of them are our own people, and we ought to shew an equal respect to all."[33] This sentiment he amplified upon the second reading of the bill in February. Agreeing that "our sugar colonies are of great consequence to us" and that "we ought not to leave them under any hardships or under any distress"—for "let it never be said of a British House of Commons that the distress of any of their fellow-subjects was pointed out to them, and they neglected to do what was in their power for their relief"—Oglethorpe countered with a word of caution that "our other colonies in that part of the world ought also to be considered," and listed the products of those parts "which contribute not a little towards preserving the general balance of trade in our favour." Convinced

---

[33]"Cobbett's Parliamentary History of England". Volume VIII, p. 920.

that some relief should be given the sugar colonies, he nevertheless maintained that "we ought not to encourage or raise one colony upon the destruction or detriment of another; much less ought we to grant a favour to any subject, or to any particular set of people, which may prove to be against the public good of the nation in general."[34] In short, he craved imperial preference, not isolated protection. Had George III and Lord North abided by these judgments, Oglethorpe himself might never have greeted John Adams as the first American Minister to the Court of St. James. But, as Wright so neatly phrased it, "as usual he was in the minority; for the Commons had still to pass through more than a century of strife ere they were compelled to give way to the Free Trade principles which he so long anticipated."[35] Again the consequences were far-reaching, for Oglethorpe had shown no insular attitude toward imperial problems, but a far-sighted, cosmopolitan viewpoint which, as in all his parliamentary remarks, betokened a comprehensive grasp of the problems that might lie before him.

At the same time that the Sugar Colonies Bill was under consideration, a private petition came before the House which gave Oglethorpe an opportunity to encourage manufacture and industry. Thirty years before the Industrial Revolution was to begin its momentous transition in the manufacturing life of Great Britian, Sir Thomas Lombe had received a patent on a silk engine. Owing to financial and technical handicaps but recently overcome, he now presented a petition to parliament craving an extension of the patent. Despite strong opposition thereto, Oglethorpe urged its renewal as the engine was a proven success and the profit on this operation was fully fifty per cent which, he said, "is all clear money got to the nation (and) all clear gain to us, because it is added by the labour and industry of our own people." Exhibiting a logic equal to his economic theory, Oglethorpe concluded that, "since this gain can be made only by the means of this engine, we must grant that this gentleman has, at his own hazard and charge, brought home a very useful and profitable branch of trade to his own country, for which he certainly deserves a recompence."[36] To his interest in domestic public

---

[34]*Ibid.*, pp. 1000-1001.

[35]Wright, *op. cit.*, p. 136.

[36]"Cobbett's Parliamentary History of England". Volume VIII, pp. 924-925, 927-928.

economy, freedom of conscience and worship, national defence, foreign commerce and imperial policy, Oglethorpe now added a strong approval of the budding mechanical revolution in industry. He was rapidly becoming the well-rounded Member of Parliament.

Even as he had advocated protection of the rich industrial entrepreneur's investments, so he now spoke to protect the life savings of the small investor. In the last days of 1731 the "Charitable Corporation", a huge company for advancing money to the poor at low rates, suddenly collapsed. Founded in 1707 with a capital limited to £30,000, it had expanded under the guidance of leading financiers so that by 1731 its capital was £600,000. The disappearance, in October of that year, of both the cashier and warehouse-keeper alarmed the proprietors who, demanding an investigation, found but £30,000 on hand. The shareholders, many of whom were thus reduced to poverty, petitioned the Commons for redress. Oglethorpe, "whose ears", as Wright justly claimed, "were ever open to the cry of the oppressed",[37] seconded the motion for an investigation[38] and was elected to the committee of twenty-one.[39] In the ensuing debate, in which it was hinted that redress might be avoided by the use of legal technicalities, he strongly denounced those members who, on such slight technicalities, would have refused even to receive the petition of the unfortunates. Expressing his approval of the fundamental principles underlying such a corporation, whether called charitable or not, for "the design was . . . in itself good and useful," he asserted that "the better the design was, the more those persons deserve to be punished, who by their frauds have disappointed the people of reaping the benefit which might have accrued by an honest and faithful execution of so good an undertaking." He was therefore, "persuaded that this Petition will be received in a manner deserving of the unhappy case of the sufferers, and of the justice of this House."[40]

---

[37]Wright, *op. cit.*, p. 41.

[38]"Egmont Diary". Volume I, p. 219. February 3, 1732.

[39]Hist. MSS. Com. Volume 42. Fifteenth Report. Appendix. Part VI. "The Manuscripts of the Earl of Carlisle", p. 89. Col. the Hon. Charles Howard to Lord Carlisle. February 12, 1732.

[40]"Cobbett's Parliamentary History of England". Volume VIII, pp. 939-940. As to the "Charitable Corporation", see Nicholls, Sir George. "A History of the English Poor Law". New edition. Three volumes. London. 1904. Volume II, pp. 23-24.

Turning now to constitutional questions he opposed an amendment
to the Qualification Bill, whereby Members of the Parliament must
swear to their qualifications, not at the time and place of election, but at
the Speaker's table. He not only opposed it "as being contrary to the ancient constitution of England," but he reverted to the representative idea
in Athenian democracy when he avowed that "he wished there were no
qualifications at all, but that the country might send up who they
pleased, good sense and loyalty not being confined to fortune or estates,
but to parts and education."[41] The quondam Jacobite was boldly pre-
saging the reform bill liberal of the nineteenth century.

Except for opposition to a bill voiding certain sales by trustees of
forfeited estates, which Egmont admits Oglethorpe attacked to protect
a relation by the name of Sutton,"[42] an unworthy act on his part, this
ended the major portion of his parliamentary career. Other plans drew
him at intervals away from England, so that, while he retained his seat
until 1754, his long absences dimmed his influence and during his last
twenty years in the House he spoke but little.

In 1734 Oglethorpe faced a contest for his seat in parliament. The
Speaker of the House informed Egmont, according to the latter's diary,
that "he had great difficulty to secure Mr. Oglethorpe's election at Haslemere, but, cost what it would, he would do it though he disobliged
many friends thereby." The Speaker's influence prevailed and on June 13
Oglethorpe, despite his absence from England, was returned by his
constituency.[43]

The next year, during his visit to England, Oglethorpe debated on
the number of seamen desired for the current year. The Master of the
Rolls, craving economy, had asked a reduction from 30,000 to 20,000.
Oglethorpe, fighting successfully for the larger number, replied caus-
tically "that as to the expense, if 'twas necessary and we could not afford
it, we must cease to be a nation; and that if we had a less Naval Force in
the West Indies, and a quarrel with France, all our plantations would

---

[41]"Egmont Diary". Volume I, p. 244. March 23, 1732.

[42]*Ibid.*, p. 248. March 30, 1732; p. 261. April 24, p. 266. May 2; p. 271. May
6, 1732.

[43]*Ibid.*, Volume II, p. 62. March 16, 1734. For date see Nichols, John. "Literary
Anecdotes of the Eighteenth Century". Volume II, p. 20 note.

soon fall a prey to them; which would sink the value of all the lands in the nation 20 per cent."[44] The colonial economist here justified his doctrine of preparedness. On other matters in this session he supported the administration, "for the first time"[45] on the reply to the king's speech,[46] and again on the bill for limiting the number of officials to sit in the Commons.[47]

His sole speech of importance in 1737 dealt with the Edinburgh riots. Here he opposed the administration's bill of punishment as entirely too severe, for it was "neither calculated to punish those who were negligent in suppressing that late riot, nor for preventing the like in time to come; and I could wish that gentlemen would fall upon some other means for answering both these ends."[48] The next year he left England for an absence of five years.

While he was thus again away came the third and most painful contest in 1741, when his candidacy encountered opposition in the person of young Lord Percival, son of his bosom friend, the Earl of Egmont. When the youth impetuously claimed that his supporters "had 43 sure votes and the whole number are but 69," Egmont, according to his diary, "told him I was very sorry for it, because he would fling out Col. Oglethorpe, for whom I profest [sic] friendship. He replied, he for that reason had not acquainted me with it: that he had offered to join with Col. Oglethorpe, but his friends refused, and after all, it was as good he should be elected as another, for they had been hawking the borough, and if he had not stood, another would, for the Colonel's managers, who are two attorneys, had received the money given at former elections, and divided nothing to the electors but sunk it in their own pockets. That he agreed for a sum, but no purchase, no pay."[49] Percival later claimed that

---

[44]Hist. MSS. Com. Volume 42. Fifteenth Report. Appendix. Part VI. "The Manuscripts of the Earl of Carlisle", p. 150. Sir Thomas Robinson to Lord Carlisle. February 10, 1735. Also "Cobbett's Parliamentary History of England". Volume IX, pp. 691 and 720.

[45]Ibid., p. 147. Sir Thomas Robinson to Lord Carlisle. January 30, 1735.

[46]Cobbett's Parliamentary History of England". Volume IX, p. 677.

[47]Ibid., pp. 967-968.

[48]Ibid., Volume X, p. 307.

[49]"Egmont Diary". Volume III, p. 188. February 5, 1741.

he was opposing, not Oglethorpe, but his colleague, Peter Burrell,[50] when a compromise offer was rejected,[51] but with the nullification of the Westminister elections in London due to fraud, Percival was there chosen in the reballoting, thus yielding Haslemere to Oglethorpe.[52] Interesting light is shed on contemporary campaign expenses by a prevalent rumour that Percival went about saying that Oglethorpe had paid him £800 to retire from the Haslemere contest. In Egmont's own words, his son's opposition "was very unlucky" in the eyes of Oglethorpe's friends "for it cost Mr. Oglethorpe £1200, and £900 of it more than it needed have done if my son had not molested him."[53] Thus for a second time, despite his absence, Oglethorpe retained his seat.

Walpole fell from power in 1742. Soon afterward Henry Pelham acquired a stronger hold than even Walpole had gained. With the Whigs in absolute control and minus the internal strife which had marked much of the Walpole régime, few dared to oppose the administration. Among these "die-hards" was Oglethorpe who, although hailed by a contemporary as "a gentleman of unblemished character, brave, generous, and humane,"[54] was nevertheless consigned by Horace Walpole to a niche among "the sad refuse of all the last oppositions."[55] Burdened with inordinate garrulity and an "exceedingly shrill voice, which could be heard in the lobby, when he was speaking in the House,"[56] Oglethorpe was no longer able to hold the attention of his colleagues.[57] Horace Walpole, who as late as 1751 was uncertain whether the member for Haslemere was a Whig or a Jacobite, was "very certain

---

[50]*Ibid.*, p. 190. February 11.

[51]*Ibid.*, 191-194. February 11-14.

[52]*Ibid.*, p. 219. May 8, p. 234. December 31, 1741.

[53]*Ibid.*, p. 244. January 19, 1742.

[54]Smollett, Tobias. "History of England". Five volumes. London. 1812. Volume II, p. 503.

[55]Walpole, Horace. "Memories of the Last Ten Years of the Reign of George the Second". Two volumes. London. 1822. Volume I, p. 190.

[56]Nichols, John. *op. cit.* Volume II, p. 21, note.

[57]Walpole, Horace. *op. cit.* Volume I, p. 121.

that he was a troublesome and tiresome speaker, though even that was now and then tempered with sense."[58] Oglethorpe thus became a rather passive opponent during his last years in parliament.

His final major parliamentary battle dealt appropriately with the good of the army. In the debate on the Mutiny Bill in 1750 he spoke for parliamentary revision of mutiny cases. Taking first the part of the officers he upheld their right of honourably refusing to tell how each had voted in a court-martial, for the House of Lords was not a court of justice.[59] Concerning complaints he opposed the doctrine that "this House is never to take notice of the complaints made by the army or by any man, or any sort of men, in the army. I hope both the officers and soldiers of the army are all subjects of Great Britain; and it is our duty to take notice of every complaint made to us by any British subject, unless upon the face of it, it appears to be frivolous or unjust. Nay farther, as we are the great inquest of the nation, it is our duty to enquire diligently if any of the subjects of Great Britain be exposed to, or labouring under any and what oppressions, and to take the most effectual method for procuring them relief." This duty, he felt, should be more frequently attended to, "especially with regard to that part of the British subjects who serve in our armies either by sea or land; for they are by the nature of the service more exposed to oppression than any other part of his majesty's subjects, and it is likewise much more dangerous for them to complain." Taking now the side of the common soldier who "has common understanding as well as other men" and who would not abuse the right of protest or complaint, Oglethorpe attacked the preservation of tyranny in the army which encouraged brutal officers to use the soldiers ill by refusing them parliamentary investigations. "I shall always be jealous of a power, the exercise whereof is trusted to the absolute and arbitrary will of a single man; nor do I think that any such power can ever be necessary in time of peace; for though in time of war such a power must often be granted, yet even then it ought to be as little made use of as possible."[60] The erst-

---

[58]*Ibid.*, p. 98.

[59]"Cobbett's Parliamentary History of England". Volume XIV, pp. 622, 638-641.

[60]*Ibid.*, pp. 666-669.

while Jacobite had developed a healthy opposition to intrenched bureaucracy.

At this same time a bill for limiting the time of military service gave him an opportunity to renew the expression of his views of twenty years before, when he advocated the granting of discharges to the soldiers so that the troops in the colonies would settle as servants or tradesmen in that part of the world, thereby increasing the white population of the sugar colonies and serving as protection against the French navy.[61] This interest in the soldiers' welfare and colonial protection was his valedictory, for in 1754 he was at last defeated for re-election.

In his long parliamentary career Oglethorpe had thus expressed intelligent and timely opinions on a wide range of important subjects. Political problems, however, had not been his sole interest. He was inveigled into at least one quarrel,[62] but this was more than balanced by two examples of his humanity. In 1728 he produced a pamphlet, entitled "The Sailor's Advocate", in which he courageously exposed the evils of impressment and the abuses countenanced by the Admiralty. If the adoption of Oglethorpe's colonial policy might have prevented the American Revolution, can it not with equal justice be claimed that, had Britain in 1728 accepted his views on impressment, the War of 1812 might at least in part have been avoided? The other effort was his activity in the cause of freedom. In January, 1731 Oglethorpe had been chosen a Director or Assistant of the Royal African Company,[63] and the next year was elected Deputy Governor.[64] As such he became interested in the negro to the extent that, when in 1733 Job Jalla, an African slave, escaped from Maryland to England, Oglethorpe provided funds for his sustenance[65] until he was returned to Africa as a freedman by the Royal African

---

[61]*Ibid.*, pp. 758-759.

[62]Hist. MSS. Com. Volume 29. Fifteenth Report. Appendix. Part IV. Portland MSS. Volume VII. Harley Letters and Papers. Volume V. p. 427. Rev. Dr. Stratford, Canon of Christ Church, Oxford, to Edward Harley. February 23, 1726.

[63]"Gentleman's Magazine". Volume I. 1731, p. 27.

[64]*Ibid.* Volume II. 1732, p. 584.

[65]Nichols, John. "Literary Anecdotes". Volume V, p. 91.

Company in 1736.[66] The next year Oglethorpe was made a Governor of Westminster Infirmary,[67] and in 1738 began his interest in letters which led to his great friendship in old age with Samuel Johnson and Boswell.[68]

It is evident from this survey of the parliamentary period of his life that Oglethorpe had, as early as 1730, established a reputation both as a leader among the opposition and as a humanitarian interested in eleemosynary activities. It was therefore, but natural that he should assume a major part in a new movement which was to unite within itself the two great interests in his public career: Philanthropy and the Welfare of the Empire. This movement was the founding of Georgia.

---

[66]"Gentleman's Magazine". Volume VI. 1736, p. 681.

[67]"Egmont Diary". Volume II, pp. 455, 458 and 464. December, 1737.

[68]Boswell, *op. cit.*, p. 25. See also Nichols, John. "Illustrations of the Literary History of the Eighteenth Century". Eight volumes. London. 1817-1858. Volume V, p. 166.

IV

The Georgia project grew out of the alliance of two separate forces. The first was the force of ideals as manifested in philanthropy, ideals which, contends Professor E. D. Adams, have influenced the progress of America more than "the economic man".[1] The second was that of which Doyle wrote when he asserted that, "if the eighteenth century was the age of Addison and Horace Walpole, it was in a far more abiding sense the age of Chatham and Wolfe and Clive":[2] the force of empire.

The prison inquiry had put an end to many great evils, but no provision had been made for "the miserable wretches . . . let out of Gaol" by the Act of 1729, people who, as Oglethorpe told Egmont, were "starving about the town for want of employment."[3] To remedy this situation by relieving London of its surplus unemployed, Oglethorpe conceived the idea of sending a hundred or more of these people, as the diary records, to "the West Indies",[4] meaning America.[5] The money for this project came from two direct gifts, and later from another collateral source. A haberdasher named King having died, his estate of £15,000

[1]Adams, E. D., "The Power of Ideals in American History". Dodge Lectures in Citizenship. Yale University. New Haven. 1913, pp. xii-xiii.

[2]Doyle, *op. cit.*, p. 418.

[3]"Egmont Diary". Volume I, p. 45. February 13, 1730.

[4]*Ibid.*, p. 90. April 1, 1750.

[5]Crane, Verner W. "The Philanthropists and the Genesis of Georgia". American Historical Review. Volume XXVII, No. 1. October, 1921, p. 66, n.

was entrusted to three trustees. One of them desiring to convert it illegally, the other two retained Oglethorpe to aid them in the fulfillment
of their duties. As a reward for winning their lawsuit for them, Oglethorpe received a grant of £5,000 for his enterprise, to be added to such
other sums as he could provide.[6] In accordance with the terms of this
grant, Oglethorpe now sought further funds and found another important source.

The Reverend Thomas Bray, founder of the Society for the Pro-
motion of Christian Knowledge and of the Society for the Propagation
of the Gospels, and quondam missionary to Maryland, was interested
in numerous philanthropies, among which was the Christian education
of negroes. For this purpose he had acquired a gift of £900 from M.
Asbel Tassin, sieur d'Allone. In 1723 ill health made Bray anxious for
the perpetuation of these benevolences so that he organized the Associates of Dr. Bray, naming among his trustees John, Viscount Percival,
later Earl of Egmont, Oglethorpe's colleague on the prison committee.
Through their common interest in imprisoned debtors, Oglethorpe had
met both Bray and Percival. Here was his opportunity. To the former's
fund from the d'Allone gift he now added the King legacy. On Bray's
death in February, 1730, Oglethorpe was made a trustee of his estate, so
that by June, 1730, the programme awaited merely parliamentary aid
for its successful inception.[7] Each step in James Oglethorpe's parliamentary career had thus contributed to the evolution of this project, but
even as it was maturing in his fertile mind, the course of events, in distant climes as well as in Westminster, had created the complementary situation which made possible the fulfillment of Oglethorpe's dreams.

At the opening of the eighteenth century there lay on the eastern
coast of North America a narrow chain of English colonies extending

---

[6]Roberts, R. A. "The Birth of an American State: Georgia: An Effort of Philanthropy and Protestant Propaganda". Transactions of the Royal Historical Society.
Fourth Series. Volume VI. London. 1923, pp. 24-25.

[7]Crane, op. cit., p. 63. For Bray's work, see article in Dictionary of National
Biography. Volume VI, p. 240; Tiffany, C. C. "A History of the Protestant Episcopal
Church in the United States of America". New York. 1895. pp. 65-70, 278-279;
McConnell, S. D. "History of the American Episcopal Church". New York. 1890.
Chapters IX-X, pp. 96-112, passim. As to Oglethorpe, see "Egmont's Diary". Volume
I, p. 99.

from Massachusetts in the north to Carolina in the south. Although internally cemented by the Restoration conquest of New York from the Dutch and the expulsion of the Swedes from the Delaware, these colonies faced, on their frontiers, not only the Indians but also the colonists and claims of other European nations. Carolina, the southern border, lay unprotected against depredatory raids of both the Indians and the hostile Spaniard[s], for nigh two centuries ensconced in Florida. Farther to the west the French had established in Louisiana the lower point of a crescent which, rising through the Mississippi and Ohio Valleys to Canada, created a barrier to westward expansion of the English colonies that was not broken until Wolfe met Montcalm on the Heights of Abraham in 1759 and a young Virginian by the name of George Washington helped to win the Ohio Valley.

The Yamassee Indian War in 1715-1716 made it quite manifest that Carolina needed the protection of a buffer state on its southern border as well as a determination of boundaries in a debatable territory wherein the English now established a fort.[8] In 1717 Sir Robert Montgomery, son of a Nova Scotian baronet who with others had failed in an earlier attempt to colonize southern California, put forth a prospectus entitled "A Discourse concerning the designed establishment of a New Colony to the South of Carolina, the most delightful country in the Universe". Herein he proposed the creation of "the Margravate of Azilia" between the Savannah and Altamaha rivers, whose chief purpose, according to Osgood, was "that it would be a barrier against the Spanish and Indians."[9] At the same time it was proposed that the Carolina proprietors should surrender their rights to the crown, which, however, was declined. As Stevens so keenly analyzed it, the Margravate "was magnificent upon the map, but was impracticable in reality". The proposals, "though garnished with the most glowing descriptions, . . . were issued in vain,"[10] Montgomery's programme failed, and the southern border of Carolina continued unprotected. In 1730, a year after the transition

[8]Bolton, H. E. and Marshall, T. M. "The Colonization of North America, 1492-1783". New York. 1922. p. 315.

[9]Osgood, H. L. "The American Colonies in the Eighteenth Century". Four volumes. Columbia University. New York. 1924. Volume II, p. 365.

[10]Stevens, W. B. "History of Georgia". Two volumes. 1847. Volume I, p. 59.

to a crown colony, when the province was divided into North and South Carolina, Sir Alexander Cuming succeeded in nullifying a rising French influence among the Cherokee Indians who now formally acknowledged English supremacy, but the Spanish peril remained and the British government continued to seek a sound programme of simultaneous colonial expansion and defence.

While the Colonial Office was seeking a *modus operandi*, Oglethorpe had completed his plans with Egmont. On April 1, 1730, he had decided on America for his colony; on June 26 he chose Carolina.[11] On July 1 the decision was made to use all available funds of various estates,[12] and in Egmont's diary under date of July 30 is this entry: "We agreed on a petition to the King and Council for obtaining a grant of lands on the southwest of Carolina for settling poor persons of London, and having ordered it to be engrossed fair, we signed it, all who were present, and the other Associates were to be spoke also to sign it before delivered."[13] On September 17 this petition for a charter was presented to the Privy Council where it languished for over a year and a half.[14] During this long period of suspense Oglethorpe's faith in the king and the Whig oligarchy never faltered although he and Egmont were compelled to use all their political skill in extracting from a reluctant Walpole a satisfactory charter.[15] What with securing the favour of the Board of Trade;[16] personal scruples "whether the acceptance of the government of the colony we are sending to Georgia doth not vacate our seats in Parliament" which Oglethorpe proposed to overcome by a qualifying Act of Parliament;[17] the necessity of securing Lord Carteret's approval as

---

[11]"Egmont Diary". Volume I, pp. 90 and 98.

[12]*Ibid.*, p. 98.

[13]*Ibid.*, p. 99.

[14]Hist. MSS. Com. Volume 19. Eleventh Report. Appendix. Part IV. The Townshend MSS. p. 258. Among the Papers Relating to the American Plantations in the Townshend MSS. at Raynham is "An Account of the Several Steps taken by the Privy Council upon granting the Georgia Charter."

[15]"Egmont Diary". Volume I, pp. 120-164, *passim*; especially pp. 129 and 157.

[16]*Ibid.*, p. 127. February 6, 1731.

[17]*Ibid.*, p. 129. February 9.

last of the Carolina proprietors;[18] and obtaining Walpole's promise to allow the project a share of the proceeds of the current state lottery,[19]— it was little wonder that by June 17, 1731, Oglethorpe was displeased with the first draft of the charter as submitted by the Attorney-General "who has constituted a new election of Councillors every three years which we apprehend is to take the power out of our hands and put it into new ones, who may convert the scheme into a job. He has also put the Militia of the intended colony into the single hand of the Governor of Carolina, whereby he at his pleasure may distress our people." In addition, as Egmont noted, it gave the king financial benefits which made the entire project a discouragement.[20] The two leaders successfully pleaded for revision of the charter only to find that Whig bureaucracy was delaying its release. Although the king had "put the fiat to our Carolina Charter" on January 26, 1732,[21] the Duke of Newcastle now held up its delivery[22] although Walpole blamed the king.[23] Not until the end of May did the charter finally pass the bureaux[24] to be signed by the king on June 9-20, 1732.

To Oglethorpe and nineteen associates, most of whom had been on the prison investigation committee with him,[25] was granted the status of "Trustees for establishing the colony of Georgia in America". The motives for such a grant were threefold: In the first place, domestic unemployment. "Many of our poor subjects, if they had means to defray their charges of passage . . . would be glad to settle in any of our provinces in America where by cultivating the lands, at present waste and desolate, they might . . . gain a comfortable subsistence for themselves and families." In the second place, the king, while discoursing philan-

---

[18]*Ibid.*, pp. 154-155. March 5 and 8, 1731. Also p. 278. May 30, 1732.

[19]*Ibid.*, p. 164. March 18, 1731.

[20]*Ibid.*, p. 193. June 17. Also p. 209. November 26.

[21]*Ibid.*, p. 218. January 26, 1732.

[22]*Ibid.*, p. 223. February 18.

[23]*Ibid.*, p. 226. February 25.

[24]*Ibid.*, p. 277. May 29.

[25]Crane, *op. cit.*, p. 65.

thropically, was thinking imperially, so that he hoped "they might *not only gain a comfortable subsistence* for themselves and families, *but also strengthen our colonies and increase the trade, navigation, and wealth of these our realms*." Finally he gave heed not only to imperial expansion but also to imperial defence, and sanctioned the project of a buffer state for South Carolina because "our provinces in North America have been frequently ravaged by Indian enemies; more especially that of South Carolina," which, having been previously laid waste, "will in the case of a new war be exposed (again) inasmuch as their whole southern frontier continueth unsettled and lieth open to the said savages." To this body he therefore granted, for only twenty-one years however, full rights of government by a common council of fifteen which included Oglethorpe and Egmont, the latter as president. The territory granted was that of the defunct Margravate of Azilia. In accordance with the prevailing English tenets, the charter ordained that, always excepting Roman Catholics, "forever hereafter there shall be a liberty of conscience allowed in the worship of God." After providing for colonial defence in which the governor of South Carolina was to command the Georgian militia, the charter closed with the provision for Georgia's reversion to the crown at the end of twenty-one years.[26] As McCain has shown, "the granting of such a charter was in a measure a reversion to type"; that is, to the old idea of ultimate royal control.[27]

The charter having been granted, the trustees began at once to function. As this project was to be one of "assisted emigration" as Austin Dobson has defined it,[28] particular attention was paid in the beginning to two problems: Proper publicity for the venture and the acquisition of adequate revenues, in both of which Oglethorpe played a major rôle. At the Council meeting of August 3, 1732, he was appointed publicity agent to advertise the project in all the newspapers and to censor all undesirable articles relating thereunto.[29] In the words of Professor Os-

---

[26]Text in McDonald, William. "Documentary Source Book of American History, 1606-1913". New York. 1920. pp. 95-103.

[27]McCain, J. R. "Georgia as a Proprietary Province: The Execution of a Trust". Boston. 1917. pp. 24-25.

[28]Dobson, *op. cit.*, p. 9.

[29]Candler, A. D., editor. "The Colonial Records of the State of Georgia". Atlanta, Georgia. In progress. 1904 - . Volume II, p. 3. (Hereinafter cited as "Colonial Records of Georgia".)

good, "by 1730 the newspaper and periodical press was well developed in England and its influence was enlisted on behalf of Georgia to an extent which was never dreamed of in the case of any other colony."[30] The "Gentleman's Magazine" during this formative period cited articles from the daily journals wherein the Georgia movement was compared to the old Roman concept of colonization as "among the noblest of their works."[31] In addition to this work Oglethorpe wrote "An Essay on Plantations"[32] and produced a prospectus entitled "A New and Accurate Account of the Provinces of South Carolina and Georgia" wherein he proclaimed the philanthropic purposes of the colony: "The unfortunate will not be obliged to bind themselves to a long servitude to pay for their passage, for they may be carried gratis into a land of liberty and plenty, where they immediately find themselves in possession of a competent estate in a happier clime than they knew before; and they are unfortunate indeed, if here they cannot forget their sorrows." Asserting that persons reduced to poverty were not wealth to the nation, but might be happy in Georgia and there become profitable to England, he placed such paupers within the design of the patent.[33] A nobler and more modest appeal than Montgomery's florid proclamation, this merited a more successful issue.

The greater the appeal of the project and the warmer its reception, the more necessary became increased resources. The charter had created a corporation "for the receiving, managing and disposing of the contributions of our loving subjects," but long before its formal grant by the king, Oglethorpe and Egmont had sought further funds to add to the King and d'Allone nuclei. Campaigning for subscriptions, large and small, had begun in July, 1730,[34] nor were the possibilities of a lottery

---

[30]Osgood, *op. cit.* Volume III, p. 37.

[31]Cf. "Gentleman's Magazine". Volume II. 1732. pp. 893-894. Reprint of article: "On the Colony of Georgia", in the "London Journal" of August 5, 1732. No. 684.

[32]Nichols, John. "Literary Anecdotes". Volume II, p. 17.

[33]The text can be found in "Collections of the Georgia Historical Society". Savannah. 1840. Volume I, pp. 42-78.

[34]"Egmont Diary". Volume I, p. 99. July 30-31, 1730.

overlooked.[35] But the greatest stroke of fortune was yet before the pro-
moters. In 1723 George Berkeley, who had been with Theophilus Oglethorpe in the Peterborough entourage in Sicily in 1714,[36] informed his
friend Percival of his project for a Christian College in "the sea-girt
Bermuda islands with their innocence and security" for "the reforma-
tion of manners among the English in our western plantations and the
propagation of the Gospel among the American savages."[37] On the
promise of a government grant of £20,000, Berkeley went out to Bermuda in 1728 and laboured both there and in Rhode Island for the next
three years, but, as Reverend McConnell well said, "to secure the grant
was one thing, to secure the money quite another."[38] Without it Berkeley
could do nothing. On December 23, 1730, Percival informed him of
the Georgia project: "Mr. Oglethorpe, a young gentleman of very public spirit and chairman of the late committee of gaols, gave the first hint
of this project last year, and has very diligently pursued it."[39] This
shortly led Berkeley to return, deeply disappointed at the utter lack of
support.[40] Oglethorpe now concluded that *his* project, "being entirely
calculated for a secular interest," held greater promise of governmental
support than Berkeley's missionary idea,[41] with the result that on March
10 the trustees proposed to ask the government for a share of the unpaid
£20,000.[42] Oglethorpe therefore wrote to Berkeley still in Rhode Island, asking him to aid this project in view of his own inability to acquire the grant, and promising in return the support of the trustees for

---

[35]*Ibid.*, p. 164. March 18, 1731.

[36]Rand, Benjamin. "Berkeley and Percival: The Correspondence of George
Berkeley, afterwards Bishop of Cloyne, and Sir John Percival, afterwards Earl of Egmont". Cambridge University Press. 1914. pp. 19-20, 130.

[37]*Ibid.*, p. 203. Berkeley to Percival. London. March 4, 1723.

[38]McConnell, *op. cit.*, p. 133. See also Tiffany, *op. cit.*, pp. 282-286; Rand, *op.
cit.*, pp. 31-43, 203, 230.

[39]Rand, *op. cit.*, pp. 269-272. Percival to Berkeley. Bath. December 23, 1730.

[40]*Ibid.*, pp. 273-274. Berkeley to Percival. Rhode Island. March 2, 1731.

[41]*Ibid.*, p. 270 and *passim*; Crane, *op. cit.*, pp. 63-69, *passim*.

[42]"Egmont Diary". Volume I, p. 157. March 10, 1731. Also Rand, *op. cit.*, p.
274.

his future projects.[43] Berkeley's reply was to return to England on October 30, and the next day repair to Egmont's home[44] where he and Oglethorpe engaged in lengthy conferences.[45] The result of these meetings was a motion in Parliament in May, 1732, for a grant of £10,000, whose ultimate success was aided by an uncommon amount of vagrancy in London at that time, of which Oglethorpe took prompt advantage.[46] The granting of the charter now opened the purses of the financial interests. Upon this royal recommendation the directors of the Bank of England subscribed £300, while the East India Company directors gave £600, so that by September 14, 1732, over £2,000 had been gathered together.[47]

Oglethorpe had given the project such wide publicity that, when the charter opened the way for the first expedition to Georgia, the trustees had received applications not only from domestic paupers but also from Swiss emigrationists and the Salzburg Protestants whom he had befriended a short time before, in Parliament.[48] In July the trustees, although feeling the moment not yet propitious for departure, had selected the personnel of the first party, made up of ambitious English paupers,[49] when Oglethorpe made an offer which was to change the entire course of both his own life and the Georgia project.

On June 19 had died his old mother, Lady Eleanor Wall Oglethorpe, leaving her distinguished son without any domestic ties or encumbrances to check his future career.[50] He now determined to cast his lot with the Georgia pioneers. This offer, in Jones' approbative words,

[43]Rand, *op. cit.*, pp. 275-279. Oglethorpe to Berkeley. May, 1731.

[44]"Egmont Diary". Volume I, p. 207. November 1, 1731. Rand, *op. cit.*, pp. 43 and 279.

[45]E.g., "Egmont Diary". Volume I, p. 214. January 12, 1732. Rand, *op. cit.*, p. 279.

[46]"Egmont Diary". Volume I, pp. 273-274. May 11-12, 1732.

[47]*Ibid.*, p. 292. September 14, 1732. See also the "Gentleman's Magazine". Volume II. 1732. p. 975.

[48]*Ibid.*, pp. 282 and 287. June 29 and July 27, 1732.

[49]"Gentleman's Magazine". Volume II. 1732. p. 874.

[50]*Ibid.*, Volume II. 1732. p. 827.

"placed the seal of consecration upon his self-denial, patriotism, and enlarged philanthropy,"[51] and evoked the congratulations of Thomas Penn, proprietor of Pennsylvania, and Governor Belcher of Massachusetts.[52] Attached to this offer, however, was a proviso that the first band of emigrants should sail at once. To this Egmont and many others were opposed on the grounds of unpreparedness although the former rejoiced "that Mr. Oglethorpe would go, for my great pain was that although we were ever so well prepared, it would be difficult to find a proper Governor, which post he has accepted of."[53] Oglethorpe nevertheless was adamant[54] and on October 18 the trustees, of whom but half remained interested, decided to send the party immediately.[55]

Thus it came to pass that, when, after many delays, the frigate, "Ann", set forth from Gravesend on November 17, 1732, in the quaint words of the "Gentleman's Magazine", with 116 persons and "10 tons of Alderman Parson's best beer . . . for the service of the colony," Oglethorpe was the accompanying trustee "to see them settled" in Georgia.[56]

Arriving at Charleston on January 13, 1733,[57] where they were warmly welcomed by the South Carolinians who fully appreciated the value to themselves of Georgia as a buffer state, the pioneers proceeded to their wilderness where, on a tract ceded by the Indians and lying on the banks of the Savannah river, they began to erect the town of that name. In this as in other matters Oglethorpe assumed full command for, in Dr. McKinley's trenchant words, "as so frequently the case in philanthropic enterprises, the recipients of the charity in Georgia were ex-

---

[51]Jones, C. C. "History of Georgia". Two volumes. Boston, 1883. Volume I, p. 115.

[52]Ibid., p. 131.

[53]"Egmont Diary". Volume I, p. 293. October 18, 1732.

[54]Ibid., p. 304. December 21, 1732. A reflection by Egmont on a letter from the Governor of South Carolina confirming the former's judgment as to delaying the passage of the first group. "But Mr. Oglethorpe was eager to begin the colony."

[55]Ibid., p. 293. October 18, 1732.

[56]"Gentleman's Magazine". Volume II. 1732. pp. 1029, 1079-1080.

[57]"Egmont Diary". Volume I, p. 339. February 28, 1733. Quoting from a letter by Oglethorpe to Egmont from Georgia.

pected passively to take what was given, and Oliver Twists were not included in the calculations of Oglethorpe or the other trustees."[58] His activities in the next year and a half were devoted to problems of administration: Conciliation of the neighboring Indians, and the details of domestic government, including immigration from the Continent and certain phases of what would today be called social service.

O. M. Dickerson, in his study, "American Colonial Government, 1696-1765", declares that "the friendship of the southern Indians was cultivated even more assiduously than was that of the northern ones, and presents in large quantities were regularly given to the Indians on the borders of South Carolina and Georgia."[59] Through the mediacy of Mary Musgrove, the Indian wife of a white trader, Oglethorpe met Tomochichi, the Indian chief who was to be his strongest ally in the New World. With him he concluded a convention whereby the natives surrendered a tract of land near the coast between the Savannah and Altamaha rivers, and agreed to have no communication with the French and Spaniards. Thus in the beginning of the enterprise Oglethorpe effected a measure which proved of great value in protecting the colony from Indian attacks during the critical period of its early history.[60]

The core of the problems in administration was the vital question of defence. The Indians had been pacified; the Spaniard and, to a lesser degree, the Frenchman remained. The building of fortifications to protect Savannah and a rigorous training in arms constituted his plan of defence in which he secured the hearty support of South Carolina. But for this purpose the growth of the populace was equally important, and here Oglethorpe surpassed the English conception of colonies. As G. L. Beer shows in his survey of British colonial policy, England opposed migration at this time, so that the philanthropy was that of Oglethorpe, not

---

[58]McKinley, A. E. "The Suffrage Franchise in the Thirteen English Colonies in America". Philadelphia. University of Pennsylvania. 1905. p. 163.

[59]Dickerson, O. M. "American Colonial Government". Cleveland, Ohio. 1912. p. 337.

[60]Greene, E. B. "Provincial America, 1690-1740". The American Nation Series. Volume VI. New York. 1905. p. 257. The volume in the "Colonial Records of Georgia", Volume XX, which should contain Oglethorpe's correspondence, 1733-1735, has not been published.

of the government. He therefore strove to build up Georgia with continental emigration.[61] Although the trustees had resolved not to tempt the Salzburgers to Georgia before they had first been banished from the Tyrol by the government,[62] the welcoming gestures of the Protestant princes of Germany caused them to invite these German Lutherans[63] who, under Baron von Reck and Pastor Bolzius, came over early in 1734, the first religious body to seek asylum in Georgia. Settling on Oglethorpe's advice at Ebenezer near Savannah, they lent to the colony a certain stability of honest labour, military strength and strong moral character.[64] At the same time Oglethorpe welcomed the Piedmontese silkworm cultivator, Amatis, who attempted an ill-faring project in the new colony.[65]

The manner of inviting the Salzburgers and their importance in his defensive programme caused Oglethorpe to pay particular attention to these highly-valued immigrants, attentions which were soon spread to all the colonists for, writes Osgood, "what in certain respects was superior to all this (administrative achievement), Oglethorpe mingled freely with the colonists, superintended the entire work of settlement, shared in its physical labor, cared for the sick, settled disputes, maintained discipline. In this step he was the father of the enterprise. . . ."[66] Evidences of this interest abound in the journals of the two Salzburg leaders, who recurrently record their gratitude for his manifold favours. Well they might, for he had postponed his return to England in order to welcome them, and on their arrival he had sent them bounteous provisions.[67] When therefore he left Georgia in 1734 von Reck recorded in

---

[61]Beer, G. L. "British Colonial Policy, 1754-1765". New York. 1907. pp. 133, note 134, note.

[62]"Egmont Diary". Volume I, pp. 302-303. December 21, 1732.

[63]*Ibid.*, p. 345. March 28, 1733.

[64]Strobel, *op. cit.* Passim.

[65]"Egmont Diary". Volume I, p. 344. March 21, 1733.

[66]Osgood, *op. cit.* Volume I, p. 49.

[67]"Extract of the Journals of Mr. Commissary von Reck . . . and of the Reverend Mr. Bolzius". S.P.C.K. London. 1734. Reprinted in the Peter Force Tracts. Volume IV. Washington. 1846. Especially pp. 8, 9, 11 and 26.

his journal the sorrow of the people at the departure of one "who had carefully watched over them as a good Shepherd does over his Flock, and who had had so tender a Care of them, both by Day and by Night; and they were afflicted, that the Fatigues and Difficulties of so long a Voyage left them very small Hopes of seeing Him again."[68]

Oglethorpe's position in the colony has been a subject for conflicting opinions. Despite Egmont's notation in his diary that Oglethorpe was to be "Governor",[69] Osgood claims that, "on his first visit, Oglethorpe's relations to the colony were temporary and informal. He accompanied the expedition voluntarily, paying his own expenses and taking with him no distinctly official commission."[70] McKinley admits that "it is difficult to define the authority as exercised" by him,[71] while McCain asserts that he was needed as an unofficial guiding hand, but was not expected to stay long. "He was not a governor under the Trustees, but their Attorney to act in their stead" with powers limited to specific matters.[72] In short it seems that, without due authorization, to quote Channing, "he exercised paternal power over the settlers, acting as judge, lawgiver, and defender."[73]

While Oglethorpe continued to labour in Georgia, even when at times ill—either from fever[74] or from the effects of falling from his horse among some canes, three of which entered his body,[75]—Egmont filled an equally important post at home. He it was who conceived, presented and at times well-nigh fought for the annual petitions to Parlia-

---

[68]*Ibid.*, p. 13. Von Reck Journal. March 23, 1734; p. 23. Bolzius Journal. March 16, 1734. Bolzius speaks of "Oglethorpe's Fatherly Care".

[69]"Egmont Diary". Volume I, p. 293. October 18, 1732.

[70]Osgood, *op. cit.* Volume III, p. 49. For a similar view as to "informal government" in Georgia, see Greene, E. B. "The Provincial Governor in the English Colonies of North America". New York. 1907. p. 39.

[71]McKinley, *op. cit.*, p. 164.

[72]McCain, *op. cit.*, pp. 63 and 65.

[73]Channing, E. "A History of the United States". In progress. New York. 1904-. Volume II. "A Century of Colonial History", p. 363.

[74]"Egmont Diary". Volume I, p. 372. May 9, 1733.

[75]*Ibid.*, p. 476. December 29, 1733.

ment seeking further grants in aid of the project. Throughout the history of the enterprise his diary reveals an abiding attention to the domestic details of the trust which at all times equalled and often surpassed that of his colleague in the colony.[76]

Despite numerous private contributions such as £100 from Governor Penn of Pennsylvania,[77] the constant need of money and a serious domestic situation—caused, first by an utter lack of interest on the part of numerous trustees, and second by complaints on the part of the most important of the other trustees, James Vernon, concerning "the neglect Mr. Oglethorpe shows in not corresponding with us frequently, and thereby keeping us in great ignorance of his proceedings,"[78]—beckoned Oglethorpe to England in 1734. As he had so impressed the Indians that, in the Words of Reverend Mr. Bolzius, they "honour Mr. Oglethorpe as their Father, and ask his Advice in all their circumstances,"[79] he brought with him, in June of that year, Tomochichi and a number of his subjects whose presence became a potent though mute factor in further parliamentary appropriations.[80] Small wonder was it that on their departure for Georgia Tomochichi said he was glad to return home, but to part with Oglethorpe "was like the day of death".[81] Oglethorpe himself was welcomed both now and again in 1737 "with odes and ascriptions not only from the pen of Pope[82] and Thomson,[83] but in

---

[76]*Ibid.*, Volume I-III. *Passim.*

[77]*Ibid.*, Volume I, p. 372. May 9, 1733.

[78]*Ibid.*, Volume II, p. 41. March 3, 1734.

[79]"Bolzius' Journal", p. 22. March 15, 1734.

[80]"Egmont Diary", p. 112, June 24, 1734; p. 114, July 3. Also "Gentleman's Magazine". Volume IV, 1734. p. 329. For a Latin poem by Richard West on the visit of the Indians to Eton, see Toynbee, Paget. "The Correspondence of Gray, Walpole, West and Ashton". Two volumes. Oxford. 1915. Volume II, pp. 303-306.

[81]"Egmont Diary". Volume II, p. 132. November 4, 1734. Roberts, in his Royal Historical Society paper, p. 45, suggests that Tomochichi, though never in Ireland, must have kissed the Blarney Stone.

[82]Written in 1737. "Imitations of Horace". See page 2, note 1, supra; also Nichols. "Literary Anecdotes". Volume II, p. 23, note, for full quotation. In Austin Dobson's opinion these lines have "done more to preserve the memory of the founder of Georgia than all the records of the Office at Westminster". Dobson, *op. cit.*, p. 17.

[83]"Liberty". Part V. Verses 638-646. For full quotation see Nichols, *op. cit.* Volume II, p. 23, note.

terms of most extravagant eulogy from many an anonymous writer in the public prints,"[84] much of which found its way into the "Gentleman's Magazine".[85] At this time also the Town Council of Inverness made him a burgess by proxy,[86] and his head was proposed by Sylvanus Urban of the "Gentleman's Magazine" as a prize medal,[87] so that, in McCain's words, "his one year of labors in Georgia had gained for him more consideration and honor than he could have won from decades of service in Parliament or from a whole life of mingling in the society of the times."[88]

Oglethorpe's return had, temporarily at least, revived the falling attendance at trustees' meetings,[89] so that largely at his instigation the board now enacted the most vital three laws in the proprietary history of Georgia. In accordance with his views expressed in Parliament in 1730, he now renewed his adherence to temperance in supporting the law to prohibit the sale of rum in Georgia, although he by no means avowed the doctrine of total prohibition of alcoholic stimulants. In urging the enactment of the second law, that prohibiting negro slavery, James Oglethorpe, the director and Deputy Governor of the Royal African Company and emancipator of Job Jalla, became a forerunner of Abraham Lincoln.[90] The third measure to receive his approval, one which regulated peaceful dealings with the Indians, provided for a system to license traders which was later to cause inter-colonial strife with

---

[84]Osgood, *op. cit.* Volume III, p. 37.

[85]E.g., Volume IV. 1734. p. 505. "To the Honourable James Oglethorpe. On his Return from Georgia".

[86]Stevens, *op. cit.* Volume I, p. 127.

[87]"Gentleman's Magazine". Volume V. 1735. p. 778. See also Volume VI. 1736. p. 99.

[88]McCain, *op. cit.*, p. 71.

[89]"Egmont Diary". Volume II, p. 112. June 21, 1734.

[90]It is interesting to note, however, that white servitude remained a practice in Georgia after it had passed in the other colonies. See Osgood, *op. cit.* Volume II, p. 486.

South Carolina.[91] As Osgood concludes, "these expressed to the full the
idealism which animated him, but they were so far in advance of conditions at the time and place as to be unpractical and to serve mainly as
subjects of controversy."[92]

News of an insurrection in Georgia hastened Oglethorpe's
departure[93] and he left for Cowes in October, 1735, but, owing to contrary winds, was unable to set sail for Georgia until early December.[94]
The voyage was noteworthy for the constant care which he took of his
protégés for, from the moment the ship left Cowes, the passage was most
unpleasant. As John Wesley's journal records, "the Waves of the Sea
were mighty and raged horribly. They rose up to the Heavens above,
and clave down to Hell beneath,"[95] while Oglethorpe, a convalescent
himself,[96] watched through the long hours of the night at the side of
some sick emigrant.[97] This was but one of the reasons why the colonial
records of Georgia abound in letters by the colonists eulogizing his vast
humanity whether on surging seas or in the forest primeval.[98]

If the first period was noteworthy for problems in administration,
the second was equally so in the sphere of religion. What little is known
of Oglethorpe's personal faith is found in his works, his recurrent

---

[91]For the three measures, see "Colonial Records of Georgia". Volume I, pp. 31-
55. Also "Egmont Diary". Volume II, p. 171. April 23, 1735.

[92]Osgood, *op. cit.* Volume III, pp. 49-50.

[93]"Egmont Diary". Volume II, p. 172. April 30, 1735; p. 183. June 25, 1735.

[94]*Ibid.*, pp. 200-209. October 14-December 6, 1735.

[95]"John Wesley's Journal". Third edition. Bristol. 1765. Part I, p. 6. January
25, 1736.

[96]"Egmont Diary". Volume II, p. 212. December 10, 1735; "Colonial Records
of Georgia". Volume XXI, p. 51. Oglethorpe to Verelst, Accountant for the Trustees.
Cowes. December 3, 1735.

[97]Moore, Francis. "A Voyage to Georgia in 1735". Collections of the Georgia
Historical Society. Volume I. 1840. pp. 79-152, especially p. 88. Also "Gentleman's
Magazine". Volume VI. 1736. p. 229. Letter from Savannah. February 14, 1736.

[98]"Colonial Records of Georgia". Volumes XXI-XXV. *Passim.*

expressions of devout trust in, and deep gratitude to, the Almighty[99] and the testimony of Reverend Mr. Bolzius in Georgia that "from what Knowledge we have of Him, we conclude that He hath a great Esteem for God's holy Word and Sacraments, and a great Love for God's Servants and Children, and wishes to see the Name of Christ glorified everywhere."[100] Certain it is that his magnanimity toward Anglicans and non-conformists alike was convincing evidence of his spirituality.

Religion had been accepted as a bulwark of the colony,[101] and a large body of Anglicans had grown up in Georgia, which, together with the nature of the colony gave the Established Church its usual favoured position,[102] but the first minister, Reverend Henry Herbert, had remained but three months, returning to die in England,[103] while the second, Reverend Samuel Quincy, in Tiffany's words, "had not . . . the stamina of a pioneer missionary"[104] and after a futile effort of two years fled precipitously to South Carolina.[105] Through Doctor Burton, Pres-

---

[99]"Collections of the Georgia Historical Society. Volume III. 1873. Letters of James Oglethorpe. p. 3. To Verelst. Cowes Road. November 19, 1735; p. 13. To the Trustees. Frederica, Georgia. February 13, 1736; p. 23. To Reverend Mr. Bolzius. Frederica. March 16, 1736. See further in "Colonial Records of Georgia". Volume XXI, p. 51. Oglethorpe to Verelst. Cowes. December 3, 1735; pp. 52-53. Oglethorpe to Verelst. The Needles. December 10, 1735; p. 79. Bolzius to——. Ebenezer. February 28, 1736.

[100]"Bolzius' Journal", p. 26. March 23, 1734. See also "Collections of the Georgia Historical Society". Volume III, p. 23. Oglethorpe to Bolzius. Frederica. March 16, 1736.

[101]"Egmont Diary". Volume I, p. 284. July 9, 1732. Sunday. Egmont "communicated . . . and took a certificate thereof, it being necessary upon the passing [of] our charter of Georgia". See also the "Gentleman's Magazine". Volume III, 1733. pp. 413-415. Reprint from the "Weekly Miscellany". August 11, 1733. No. 35. Letter on "Religion in Georgia". The writer hopes "that a better Face of Religion will be preserv'd in Georgia than appears in many of our American Settlements."

[102]Cross, A. L. "The Anglican Episcopate and the American Colonies". Harvard Historical Studies. Volume IX. New York. 1902. Chapters III-IV. *Passim.*

[103]Tiffany, *op. cit.*, p. 250.

[104]*Ibid.*, p. 251.

[105]Osgood, *op. cit.*, Volume III, p. 109.

ident of Corpus Christi College, Oxford, and a Georgia Trustee,[106] Oglethorpe now met three young Oxonian theologians who agreed to accompany him to Georgia to minister to both colonists and Indians. These missionaries were Charles Wesley, scholar of Christ Church; his brother, John, of Lincoln College; and Benjamin Ingham of the Queen's College.[107] Their purpose, in John Wesley's words, was "to save our souls"[108] by preaching the Gospel to the heathen.[109] Charles Wesley went out as Secretary for Indian Affairs,[110] while his brother and Ingham planned to convert the Indians.[111] The story of the Wesleys in Georgia is not a pleasant one despite Oglethorpe's efforts to help them. Charles Wesley arrived in Frederica on March 9, 1736 where, according to his journal, "Mr. Oglethorpe received me very kindly".[112] His regard for the latter changed, however, when he found himself merely the private secretary engaged day after day in writing letters. The malevolent tongues of two Frederica women completed the breach which was not healed by a hasty visit of John Wesley to the scene of conflict.[113] On July 25, within five months of his arrival in Georgia, Charles Wesley briefly

---

[106]"Egmont Diary". Volume II, p. 184. July 2, 1735. Deciding to dismiss the clergyman in Georgia as unfit, and in league with the malcontents, "Dr. Hales proposed enquiring at Lincoln College for a proper man to send in his room." See also Tyerman, L. "Life and Times of the Rev. John Wesley". Three volumes. London. 1870. pp. 109-110; Southey, Robert. "Life of Wesley". Two volumes. New York. 1874. Volume I. Chapter III.

[107]Stevens, *op. cit.* Volume I, pp. 340-341.

[108]"John Wesley's Journal". Third edition. Bristol. 1765. Part I, p. 1.

[109]"Egmont Diary". Volume II, p. 194. September 17, 1735; Tyerman, *op. cit.*, Volume I, p. 115.

[110]"Colonial Records of Georgia". Volume II, p. 123; "Egmont Diary". Volume II, pp. 195-196. September 24, 1735.

[111]"Gentleman's Magazine". Volume V. 1735. p. 617; "Egmont Diary". Volume II, p. 200. October 14, 1735.

[112]"The Journal of the Rev. Charles Wesley". Telford edition. Finsbury Library. 1909-1910. p. 7.

[113]*Ibid.*, pp. 9-65, *passim*; also Telford, J. "Life of the Rev. Charles Wesley". Revised edition. London. 1900. pp. 49-52.

noted in his journal, "I resigned".[114] The next day he left for England. If feminine gossip and slander caused Charles Wesley's break with Oglethorpe, the advice of other men in an *affaire du coeur* put an end to his brother's labours in Georgia. His Indian mission forbidden for fear of French attacks,[115] John Wesley became pastor of Christ Church, Savannah, where as a High Church ritualist, he was sadly out of place on the frontier, than which "no place more ill adapted to his rubrical rigor could have been found." As McConnell further declares, "he quickly estranged his people by his malapropos zeal,"[116] and as Tiffany avows, "the incessant attendance required by him at meetings and prayers and sermons tended inevitably to formalism and hypocrisy (for) men declined so great a usurpation over their consciences."[117] He forgot that there were in Georgia not only Anglicans, but also Protestant non-conformists as well as some Jews who had been illegally transported and whom Oglethorpe was powerless to eject.[118] Although prohibiting the Indian mission, Oglethorpe aided Wesley whenever he could as in ordering Sunday to be set apart as a Holy Day, so that when he was absent he was missed by one who needed his support so very much.[119] The climax of John Wesley's Georgian career was reached during Oglethorpe's absence in England, in 1737, when his unfortunate romance brought his mission to an abortive conclusion in the Hopkey-Williamson case. Although Oglethorpe had done his best to help on his courtship of Miss Hopkey in an affair which Tyerman calls "painfully ludicrous",[120] Wesley, accepting the advice of others not to marry, was unable to bear with composure the prompt marriage of the young lady in question to a Mr. Williamson, whereupon he repelled the bride from the communion service, thereby exposing himself to an eventual warrant for arrest. Deem-

---

[114]"Journal of the Rev. Charles Wesley", p. 66.

[115]McConnell, *op. cit.*, p. 162.

[116]*Ibid.*, p. 163; Tyerman, *op. cit.*, p. 131.

[117]Tiffany, *op. cit.*, pp. 251 and 253.

[118]"Egmont Diary". Volume I, pp. 463-464.

[119]"John Wesley's Journal". Part I, pp. 20, 22, 28.

[120]Tyerman, *op. cit.*, Volume I, pp. 146-147.

ing discretion the better part of valour, Wesley departed for Charleston, whence on December 22, 1737 he sailed for England.[121] Oglethorpe had done his best for Wesley as the latter freely acknowledged to him: "I bless God that ever you was born. I acknowledge His exceeding mercy in casting me into your hands. I own your generous kindness all the time we were at sea. I am indebted to you for a thousand favours here. Though all men should revile you, yet will I not."[122] But as Tiffany justly notes, "it was well for himself and the colony that his stay in Georgia was short."[123] On his return to England he presented his version of affairs in the colony to the trustees,[124] as had his brother,[125] but later he admitted that "all the time I was at Savannah I was thus beating the air."[126] In London Charles Wesley renewed his friendship with Oglethorpe[127] to such an extent that he was invited to return to Georgia, but that, perhaps fortunately, did not eventuate.[128] It seems clear that the similarity in the dogmatic character of both Oglethorpe and the Wesleys left much to be desired.

In the words of Austin Dobson, "the Wesleys, however, are but an episode in Georgia history,"[129] and Oglethorpe in this second period found other matters of importance to consider, including the continued selection of new types of immigrants; the problem of defence; the finances of the colony; and relations with the Indians, which led to a quarrel with South Carolina.

---

[121]"John Wesley's Journal", pp. 42-46, 62; Tyerman, *op. cit.* Volume I, pp. 143-165.

[122]Tyerman, *op. cit.*, Volume I, p. 136. Wesley to Oglethorpe. February 24, 1737. From "Wesley's Works". Volume XII, p. 39; Telford, J. "Life of John Wesley". Revised edition. London. 1899. pp. 84 and 88.

[123]Tiffany, *op. cit.*, p. 254.

[124]"John Wesley's Journal". Part II, p. 9. February 8, 1738.

[125]"Egmont Diary". Volume II, p. 312. December 8, 1736.

[126]"John Wesley's Journal". Part II, p. 27. May 24, 1738. See also Telford, J. "John Wesley", pp. 302-304.

[127]"Charles Wesley's Diary", p. 110 ff.

[128]*Ibid.*, pp. 137 and 197.

[129]Dobson, *op. cit.*, p. 21.

The factor of immigration was still closely related to that of religion in the type of continental Protestant refugee whom the trustees welcomed to Georgia. On Oglethorpe's return to England in 1734, the board had arranged for a group of Protestant Vaudois to leave their haven in Holland, and only their stubborn demand for female entail—which, having been forbidden to the English and Salzburger colonists in the past, could not now be granted to the Vaudois for fear of mutiny by the former groups—prevented their voyage to augment the population of Georgia.[130] While in England at this time, Oglethorpe had made the acquaintance of Count Zinzendorf, leader of the "Fratres Bohemiae" who, even as the Salzburgers before them, were flying from Catholic persecutions in their fatherland, the Bohemia of John Hus. David Nitschmann had accompanied Oglethorpe on his return to the colony in 1735 as a missionary to the Indians,[131] and now Zinzendorf, having persuaded Oglethorpe to grant them a site, sent a band of these Moravians from Herrnhut in Saxony to the colony[132] where from Charles Wesley they won the reputation of being "the most laborious, cheapest workers and best subjects in Georgia."[133] The Presbyterian wing of the Non-conformists now appeared in Georgia in a body of one hundred and fifty Scotch Highlanders who, in founding New Inverness, built a fort and subsequently proved a vital military asset in the defence against Spanish invasions.

Upon his return to the colony with almost three hundred immigrants, Oglethorpe decided, for purposes of both expansion and defence, to found a new town. Intent on claiming the line of the Altamaha river for imperial reasons, despite the opposition of the trustees at home,[134] he now laid out Frederica on the "wild Altama" of Goldsmith's

---

[130]"Egmont Diary". Volume I, p. 463. December 15, 1733; Volume II, pp. 42-43. March 3, 1734; p. 55. March 13; p. 75. April 3; p. 103. May 22; pp. 106-107. June 7, 1734.

[131]Osgood, *op. cit.*, Volume III, p. 109.

[132]"Egmont Diary". Volume II, pp. 132-133. November 6, 1734; pp. 140-141. January 7, 1735; p. 166. March 31, 1735.

[133]*Ibid.*, p. 313. December 8, 1736.

[134]Osgood, *op. cit.*, Volume III, p. 50.

"Deserted Village",[135] as a southern outpost against the Spaniards who had concentrated their forces at St. Augustine. This provoked the latter to renew their claims to all the territory south of the Carolinas. "The Walpole ministry," writes Greene, "strongly desired to avoid war, and in 1736 an English agent was sent to St. Augustine to settle the dispute; conferences were also held by Oglethorpe with some of the Spanish officers. No final agreement was reached, however,"[136] and preparations for defence had to be made. Although Westminster was still so scared of the Mississippi French that the government automatically granted Georgia's recurrent requests for money,[137] that danger had well nigh passed, as had the fear of the Indian. The Spaniard alone remained to become the bête noir of the Georgians. As Osgood remarks, this settlement at Frederica therefore "marks the ascendancy of military considerations in the policy of Oglethorpe in Georgia and these continued more conspicuously to absorb his attention until his career in that colony was ended."[138]

One of the important powers given to Oglethorpe on his first voyage had been to draw bills on the trustees. It was as much his failure to send vouchers with these drafts as it was his failure to keep the trustees informed of affairs that had led Vernon to commence the actions which had drawn Oglethorpe back to England in 1734.[139] In his second visit to the colony, he was given the sole right to draw bills of credit on the trustees but this time created even a worse situation than before. Admittedly allowing his military zeal to overcome his financial caution, he incurred such large expenses that, as Egmont's diary records, the trustees in sheer desperation demanded that he present his bills to the British government.[140]

---

[135]Goldsmith, Oliver. "Poems". World's Classics. Volume 123. Oxford University Press. Edited by Austin Dobson, p. 34. Line 344. Also Dobson, *op. cit.*, p. 13.

[136]Greene, E. B. "Provincial America, 1690-1740". p. 261. For truce of September, 1736, between Oglethorpe and Don Antonio de Arredondo, see "Colonial Records of Georgia". Volume XXI, pp. 225-226.

[137]"Egmont Diary". Volume II, p. 159. March 11, 1735.

[138]Osgood, *op. cit.*, Volume III, p. 51.

[139]"Egmont Diary". Volume II, p. 29. February 13, 1734; p. 41. March 3, 1734.

[140]*Ibid.*, pp. 268-293, *passim*. May 5-August 4, 1736.

The most important administrative problem of this period was one which affected the inter-colonial relations of Georgia with South Carolina. Of the three major laws approved by Oglethorpe, that prohibiting negro slavery had entailed economic disadvantage only in Georgia, where it was highly unpopular.[141] The other two, however, caused serious trouble with South Carolina. With the two colonies in much the same position as Canada and the United States today, the law prohibiting the rum trade led to such extensive rum-running and consequent enforcement of the law that a Georgian could write thus: "Our strictness in relation to the Rum Trade is like to occasion some disputes with our neighbours of Carolina. Seizures and confiscations and arrests have been made."[142] The corollary, moreover, was equally true for there is a strangely modern American touch to the evidence adduced before the trustees by a Scotch Highlander, to the effect that the people of Savannah "still get at rum, notwithstanding all our care, by means of the Carolina boats, which in the night time land it in creeks unknown to the magistrates."[143] More disastrous to the South Carolinians, however, than the prohibition of rum, was the law regulating trade with the Indians. Until the creation of Georgia, South Carolina had naturally held a monopoly in this field. On Oglethorpe's return in 1735 the trustees had appointed him "sole Commissioner to grant licenses to trade to the Indians".[144] His rigorous enforcement of the law not only destroyed the Carolinian monopoly but, by restricting this important source of profit to Georgians, virtually ruined the neighbouring traders. He had, moreover, held an important conference with the Chickasaws [*sic*] at Savannah in July, 1736,[145] and he maintained the traditional friendship with Tomochichi; all of which contributed toward nullifying Carolinian prestige

---

[141]*Ibid.*, pp. 204-205. November 12, 1735.

[142]"Gentleman's Magazine". Volume VI. 1736. p. 357. Letter from Georgia. See also the "Egmont Diary". Volume II, p. 286. June 23, 1736; p. 297. September 8, 1736.

[143]"Egmont Diary". Volume II, p. 317. December 11, 1736.

[144]"Colonial Records of Georgia". Volume II. "Minutes of the Common Council", p. 120. September 3, 1735; "Egmont Diary". Volume II, p. 195. September 24, 1735.

[145]Hist. MSS. Com. Volume 19. Eleventh Report. Appendix. Part IV. Townshend MSS., pp. 259-262.

and influence among the Indians. In vain did South Carolina complain,[146] nor was the situation eased by Charles Wesley's statement to the trustees wherein he berated the northern neighbours as "utter enemies to Georgia" who were arousing both the Spanish and Indians against the colony.[147] South Carolina was finally forced to appeal to Westminster.

The storm now broke over Oglethorpe's head. All the complainants launched their thunderbolts at the central figure in the situation. The Spanish government complained to the British authorities of his encroachments upon Spanish territory.[148] The trustees, because, in Egmont's plaintive words, they were "kept so much in the dark",[149] became so incensed at him that they sent him a letter "conceived in very strong terms, and expressing our uneasiness that we know nothing from him of the situation our affairs are in in Georgia, and so are incapacitated from answering to the complaints made against us from all quarters."[150] In London Reverend Samuel Quincy, the defunct colonial cleric, spread the tale of the malcontents[151] such as Phillip Thicknesse, who years later described himself in disgust as "one of the first fools who went over with Oglethorpe";[152] and a rumour now spread that Oglethorpe, having gained a monopoly, was privately trafficking in furs.[153] Finally, the South Carolinians themselves, infuriated by the alleged machinations of one who had been commissioned as arbitrator between their colony and Georgia,[154] hurled at him the wild charge that he was "no white man, but a subject of France who murdered all the English

---

[146]"Egmont Diary". Volume II, pp. 295-296. August 26, 1736.

[147]Ibid., p. 312. December 8, 1736; p. 318. December 15, 1736.

[148]Ibid., p. 300. October 6, 1736.

[149]Ibid., p. 302. October 13, 1736.

[150]Ibid., p. 300. October 6, 1736.

[151]Ibid., p. 294. August 18, 1736. E.g., ibid., p. 165. March 26, 1735.

[152]Hist. MSS. Com. Volume 3. Fourth Report. Papers of Lord Monboddo. p. 519. Phillip Thicknesse to Lord Monboddo. March 18, 1789. See also Nichols. "Literary Anecdotes". Volume IX, p. 257.

[153]"Egmont Diary". Volume II, p. 307. November 10, 1736.

[154]Ibid., p. 187. July 16, 1735.

he could get."[155] This avalanche of official Spanish diplomatic complaint; censure by the trustees; inane prattle of the discontented; gossip of the streets; and ridiculous revilements and calumnies of the Carolinians, marked the first real discord in Oglethorpe's colonial career.

The three issues of paramount importance to those in authority: South Carolina's appeal to Westminster; the plight of the trustees due to Oglethorpe's extravagance and neglect in correspondence; and the vital necessity of organizing a stronger defence against the Spaniard, now called him home. Late in 1736 he sailed from Georgia, still secure in the good wishes of his devoted followers.[156] After an exceedingly rough passage, in which he and another were "obliged to jump out of bed in their shirts to pull the ropes," he landed, quite fortunately in Egmont's opinion, "at Ilfracombe in Wales" on January 2, 1737.[157] He immediately proceeded to London where, after a four hour conference, he convinced Egmont of his own impeccable conduct and the salutary condition of Georgia.[158] With honeyed words and a more equable balance sheet than he had been able to exhibit on his previous visit, he next overcame the complaints of the trustees in such a decisive manner that they gave him a unanimous vote of thanks.[159] The South Carolina appeal had worried Egmont who now thought it "very fortunate that he is come before the hearing of the Carolina complaint against us, for his presence will clear up things which we were not so well instructed to speak to as we could wish."[160] With Oglethorpe present, the South Carolina appeal was now compromised by order of the privy council on the adduction of proof concerning Carolina rum-running and illicit Indian trade without the requisite Georgia licenses.[161] Two of his three prob-

---

[155]*Ibid.*, p. 315. December 11, 1736.

[156]"Egmont Diary". Volume II, p. 325. January 8, 1737; "Colonial Records of Georgia". Volume XXI, pp. 270-275. T. Causton to the Trustees. Savannah. November 26, 1736; p. 379. T. Causton to Trustees. Savannah. March 8, 1737.

[157]"Egmont Diary". Volume II, p. 325. January 7-8, 1737.

[158]*Ibid.*, pp. 325-326. January 8-9, 1737.

[159]"Gentleman's Magazine". Volume VII, 1737. pp. 58-59.

[160]"Egmont Diary". Volume II, p. 325. January 7, 1737.

[161]*Ibid.*, p. 333. January 24, 1737. See also Osgood, *op. cit.* Volume III, pp. 397-399.

lems had been settled. The third and, to Oglethorpe, the most important remained.

On January 25, 1737, Oglethorpe asked Parliament to grant him
£30,000 for a proper defence of Georgia, secretly hoping to obtain
£20,000.[162] This request created a crisis for Walpole who now sought
his advice concerning the proper measures for the security of the American colonies. Oglethorpe gave it without stint. As Egmont so interestingly reported it, "he spoke with great freedom to Sir Robert, who told
him he was not used to have such things said to him. Mr. Oglethorpe
replied, Yes, he was when he was plain Mr. Walpole; but now he was Sir
Robert, and Chief Minister, he was surrounded by sycophants and flat-
terers who will not tell him the truth." In this extraordinary conversa-
tion, Oglethorpe emphasized his earnest desire to continue the project,
but "he would and must give it up if not supported by him (Walpole),
for he had twice been overseas to carry on the Colony, and not only ven-
tured his life and health, to the neglect of his own affairs, but actually
spent 3,000*l*. of his own money." Georgia, he continued, "was a national
affair, and he did not pretend to be a Don Quixote for it, and suffer his
reputation, and he must do, if he continues his concern without public
countenance." Predicting that, if Walpole dropped Georgia, Spain
would immediately acquire it and France could attack the Carolinas and
Virginia, Oglethorpe asserted that there were only two ways in which to
defend the colonies, either by forming militia or by keeping regular
troops. He therefore asked for the power to raise a militia, which Walpole refused him. He then asked for an Inspector-General of Colonial
Forces to co-ordinate all colonial militia, to which Walpole acceded,
proposing for that post the Governor of South Carolina.[163] This being
far from satisfactory to Oglethorpe, Walpole at last agreed on March 14
to commission him General of the Forces of South Carolina and Georgia,[164] an act which went far to revive Carolina's friendship.[165] As Par-

---

[162]*Ibid.*, p. 334. January 25, 1737.

[163]"Egmont Diary". Volume II, pp. 339-340. February 6, 1737.

[164]*Ibid.*, p. 368. March 14, 1737. See also the "Gentleman's Magazine". Volume
VII, 1737. p. 371.

[165]*Ibid.*, p. 477. April 9, 1738.

liament now granted the £20,000 which he had expected,[166] Oglethorpe realized the strength of his position and refused the commission until he obtained what he originally sought, a regiment of 700 men with himself as Colonel, wherewith to defend South Carolina and Georgia.[167] Walpole now strove desperately to obtain Oglethorpe's acceptance of the governorship of South Carolina, whose people, admitting now their debt to him,[168] greatly desired Oglethorpe,[169] but, as such procedure would lose him his seat in Parliament, the latter declined to return in any capacity save solely that of military commander.[170] By June he had his regiment and had accepted his commandership-in-chief,[171] only to receive in August Walpole's request to disband his troops in order to placate Spain[172] which again had formally complained of him.[173] At this, Oglethorpe, supported by contemporary opinion,[174] "fired and asked him what man he took him to be, and whether he thought he had no conscience, to be the instrument of carrying over 3,000 souls to Georgia, and then abandoning them to be destroyed by the Spaniards, for the consideration of a regiment. He also desired to know whether Georgia was to be given up, yea or nay? If so, it would be kind and just to let the Trustees know it at once, that we might write immediately to the inhabitants to retire and save themselves in time." Walpole capitulated[175] and, despite one more weak attempt to keep him at home as a parliamentary drudge,[176] Colonel James Oglethorpe proceeded to recruit his regi-

---

[166]*Ibid.*, p. 370. March 16, 1737.

[167]"Egmont Diary". Volume II, p. 383. April 4, 1737.

[168]*Ibid.*, p. 394. April 27, 1737.

[169]*Ibid.*, p. 374. March 19, 1737.

[170]*Ibid.*, p. 401. May 7, 1737.

[171]*Ibid.*, p. 412. June 8, 1737.

[172]*Ibid.*, p. 429. August 10, 1737.

[173]"Gentleman's Magazine". Volume VII. 1737. p. 500.

[174]E.g., editorial in the London "Daily Post". August 23, 1737. Reprinted in the "Gentleman's Magazine". Volume VII. 1737. p. 500.

[175]"Egmont Diary". Volume II, p. 429. August 10, 1737.

[176]*Ibid.*, p. 434. September 21, 1737.

ment. Before allowing him to depart, however, the trustees imparted to him much good advice, drew his attention to their ever-decreasing membership, chided him for his own haphazard attendance at board meetings which they ascribed to his opposition to their new policy of retrenchments, and shunned his review of his departing regiment.[177]

Sailing at the end of June[178] for what proved to be his last visit to Georgia, Oglethorpe arrived at Frederica in September, 1738, with a regiment of soldiers and two ships suitable for naval engagements.[179] It was soon manifest that, if his first sojourn in Georgia had been devoted to the problems of administration and social amelioration, and his second had been marked by the evidences of religion, this third period was to be essentially military in character.

Before considering that phase of the subject, however, it will be well to follow the other activities in the colony to their not far distant conclusions. In the spiritual realm the final period of Oglethorpe's colonial career was notable for the passing of the Moravians, the growth of the Anglicans and Lutherans, the arrival of the Calvinists, and the zealous missionary labours of George Whitefield. To the pacific Moravians, whom Zinzendorf had sent over, as he himself told Oglethorpe, "not because they were poor, but that they might advance the Gospel,"[180] the outbreak of Spanish hostilities in 1737 [1739] proved an insurmountable barrier, and they now sought the quiet, pleasant valleys of Pennsylvania.[181] The Anglican Church, except for the activities of George Whitefield, failed to take full advantage of its favoured position. The Salzburger Lutherans, who, in contradistinction to the Moravians, proved valiant defenders of the colony, continued to progress until just before Oglethorpe's departure in 1742, when, at their request for guid-

---

[177]*Ibid.*, p. 468. February 22, 1738; p. 469. March 8, 1738; pp. 472-474. March 23, 1738; p. 475. March 30, 1738.

[178]*Ibid.*, p. 497. June 28, 1738.

[179]*Ibid.*, p. 510. December 2, 1738; Nichols. "Literary Anecdotes". Volume II, p. 20, note.

[180]"Egmont Diary". Volume II, p. 333. January 22, 1737.

[181]Osgood, *op. cit.* Volume II, pp. 504-505. [Osgood notes the outbreak of hostilities between Spanish and English in Florida as dating from 1737, but war was not officially declared until 1739. Editor's Note.]

ance, the illustrious Francke of Halle sent over Henry Melchior Muhlenberg, the future Patriarch of the Lutheran Church in America, who
thus began his historic career among the Salzburger protégés of Oglethorpe.[182] In January, 1741, the trustees sent over a band of Strasburger
Calvinists who, when asked by Egmont whether they could agree with
the Salzburger Lutherans, replied, as befitted the ancestors of the modern Reformed Church in the United States, that "the Lutherans com-
municate with a wafer, but they with bread, however, if the Minister be
a good man, they believed they should agree well."[183] The most outstanding religious character of this period, however, was George Whitefield of Pembroke College, Oxford,[184] whom Egmont proposed to the
trustees in March, 1737, for the Frederica pastorate.[185] Passing the
homeward-bound Wesley on the high seas early in the new year,[186]
Whitefield arrived on May 7 at Savannah[187] where he eschewed alike the
formalism in the church and the extraneous entangling alliances which
had proven so fatal to the Wesleys. As the latters' great labour had been
conversion, so Whitefield's *magnum opus* was the orphanage, which he
established in imitation of Hermann Francke's orphan house at
Halle,[188] and which became, according to Tiffany, the most extensive
philanthropic institution of the colonial Protestant Episcopal Church.[189]
Beginning, in Tiffany's words, "with all Wesley's vigor, but with less

---

[182]Osgood, *op. cit.* Volume II, pp. 502 and 509. See also Strobel, *op. cit. passim*;
Mann, W. H. "Life of Henry Melchior Muhlenberg". *passim*; and "Cyclopedia of
American Biography". Volume IV, p. 453. In November, 1739, Oglethorpe informed
Bolzius that he wanted, as minister at Frederica, one educated under Francke at Halle.
See "Colonial Records of Georgia". Volume XXII, Part II, p. 338. Oglethorpe to
Bolzius. Savannah. November 3, 1739.

[183]"Egmont Diary". Volume III, p. 186. January 31, 1741.

[184]Stevens, *op. cit.* Volume I, pp. 340-341.

[185]"Egmont Diary". Volume II, p. 365. March 9, 1737.

[186]Tyerman, L. "John Wesley". Volume I, p. 165; Tiffany, *op. cit.*, p. 255.

[187]Tyerman, L. "Life of the Rev. George Whitefield". Two volumes. London.
1876. Volume I, p. 122; Tiffany, *op. cit.*, p. 256.

[188]Osgood, *op. cit.* Volume III, pp. 112-113.

[189]Tiffany, *op. cit.*, p. 249.

rigor of discipline,"[190] Whitefield achieved a greater success with the people[191] despite his itinerant labours in New England and Pennsylvania, and a year in England.[192] After December, 1740, the orphan house "really became Whitefield's parish" in Tyerman's opinion,[193] and it is interesting to note that during his visit to Philadelphia in that year he declined Benjamin Franklin's suggestion to change its location. Franklin, who had a poor opinion of the personnel of the Georgia colony, "therefore refused to contribute" to the orphanage.[194] Although immersed in military problems, Oglethorpe had done what he could to help Whitefield, manifesting a particular interest in the orphanage project,[195] but the latter's complaints that trustees' orders were not carried out,[196] and that Oglethorpe's proceedings as to the orphans were arbitrary,[197] engendered much ill-will.[198] This, together with the recurrent Spanish attacks and the open hostility to Oglethorpe of the malcontents made Whitefield's labours so onerous[199] that he left Savannah on January 1, 1741,[200] for England where, upon his arrival on March 11,[201] he continued to gather funds for the orphanage.[202] In his decade of colonial

---

[190]*Ibid.*, p. 256.

[191]Tyerman, L. "George Whitefield". Volume I, pp. 130-146, *passim*.

[192]*Ibid.*, pp. 146-443, *passim*.

[193]*Ibid.*, p. 445.

[194]Franklin, B. "Memoirs". Three volumes. London, 1818. Volume I, p. 85.

[195]Cf. "Colonial Records of Georgia". Volume IV, p. 540. Letter of Oglethorpe to Thomas Jones. March, 1740.

[196]"Egmont Diary". Volume III, p. 126. April 14, 1740.

[197]*Ibid.*, p. 204. March 23, 1741. Letter by Whitefield written after his return to England that year.

[198]*Ibid.*, p. 127. April 16, 1740.

[199]Tyerman, L. "George Whitefield". Volume I, p. 447.

[200]*Ibid.*, p. 448.

[201]*Ibid.*, p. 450.

[202]*Ibid.*, pp. 542-546. For a poem to Whitefield on his departure for Georgia see the "Gentleman's Magazine". Volume VII, 1737. p. 697.

experience, therefore, Oglethorpe, despite his imperfect personal relations with their leaders, had witnessed and aided the growth of five Protestant sects, of which at least three were to radiate from their Georgian nuclei into nation-wide denominations of the modern United States.

Oglethorpe's administration of domestic affairs in Georgia had profited by the repeated criticisms of the trustees. Upon his arrival in September, 1738, he inaugurated a strict enforcement of the colonial laws and paid particular attention to safeguarding Georgia's credit, which greatly pleased the trustees.[203] Although the colonists had longed for his return,[204] two major complaints greeted him on his arrival. The first was the serious state of the colony's stores. The store-keeper, Thomas Causton, who, in Osgood's judgment, was the most important functionary at Savannah apart from Oglethorpe, was found to be running the trust heavily in debt by unauthorized expenditures. Although he was arrested and his accounts found to be in utter confusion, no proof of fraud could be found, so that the sole salutary result was to exhibit anew the slipshod methods of internal financial administration[205] and, by comparison, to nullify, to some extent at least, Oglethorpe's similar sins of omission. The latter did not gain in the esteem of the trustees by this procedure, as it was felt that he had ordered Causton's arrest merely to curry favour with the populace at their expense.[206] The other problem was that of the land question. Discouraged to begin with by the oft-times barren soil of Georgia, the colonists found a further obstacle to success in the laws of inheritance which accorded with the strictest rules of primogeniture and male [en]tail. It was this which in earlier years had brought strong protests from the Salzburgers and Scotch Highlanders; it was this which had proven the insurmountable barrier for the Vaudois; it was this which led the Scots to threaten their departure in a

---

[203]"Egmont Diary". Volume II, pp. 516-517. December 30, 1738.

[204]"Colonial Records of Georgia". Volume XXII, Part I, pp. 133-234, *passim.* Letters of colonists, November 15, 1737, to August 26, 1738; "Gentleman's Magazine". Volume IX. 1739. pp. 22-23.

[205]Osgood, *op. cit.* Volume III, p. 53. See "Colonial Records of Georgia". Volume XXII, Parts I-II.

[206]"Egmont Diary". Volume III, p. 4. January 10, 1739.

body;[207] it was this which was now to cause trouble for Oglethorpe, who was himself definitely opposed to female entail;[208] yet it continued until 1750. Nor was the problem of succession the only cause for controversy. Throughout the decade the colonists had privately grumbled at the prohibition of rum and negro slavery. With the enticing gestures of South Carolina, whose lands were more fertile, whose labour was negro slaves, and whose rum flowed freely,[209] the long-rumbling volcano of public opinion erupted. The protests became so numerous that in 1737 the trustees, in order to appease the colonists and secure information, sent over William Stephens as their secretary in Georgia.[210] In the face of Oglethorpe's continued support of the prohibitory laws, the protests which to date had come in good faith from the substantial Salzburgers as to land entail and from planters as to slavery, now appeared from the pens of a group of "malcontents" who pressed their claims in London as well as in Georgia. In 1741 three malcontents, led by Patrick Tailfer, M.D., issued an attack on Oglethorpe, entitled " A True and Historical Narrative of the Colony of Georgia in America",[211] which hurt the victim intensely and met with a sufficiently favourable reception in London to demand a reply the next year by Benjamin Martyn, the English secretary to the trustees, in "An Account, Showing the Progress of the Colony of Georgia in America from its First Establishment."[212] If the malcontents erred too much in their prejudice, Martyn, who knew nothing of conditions in Georgia, was too sanguine. The publication, in 1740, of "A State of the Province of Georgia",[213] designed to win further parliamentary appropriations despite Walpole's opposition, drew forth in 1743 a vitriolic attack on Oglethorpe by Thomas Stephens, son

---

[207]Osgood, *op. cit.* Volume III, p. 58.

[208]"Egmont Diary". Volume II, pp. 478-479. April 12, 1738.

[209]Osgood, *op. cit.* Volume III, pp. 54 and 63.

[210]"Colonial Records of Georgia". Volume IV. "Stephens' Journal, 1737-1740". Preface; "Egmont Diary". Volume II, p. 368. March 14, 1737.

[211]"Collections of the Georgia History Society". Volume II, pp. 163-264; "Egmont Diary". Volume III, p. 225. July 2, 1741; p. 229. November 14, 1741.

[212]*Ibid.*, pp. 265-310.

[213]*Ibid.*, pp. 67-86.

of the secretary in Georgia, who had an imaginary grievance against him.[214] This youth, being sent to London by the malcontents, created a crisis by his radical remarks and pro-slavery petitions.[215] Much of the propaganda cited above was unreliable and, in some cases, merely abusive, but the fact remained that, in Oglethorpe, the soldier had completely submerged the statesman. Although he still persisted in interfering at the most awkward moments, his administrative activities now became irregular, with marked effect upon affairs in general, and his powers were gradually bestowed upon, or assimilated by, other officials.[216] In 1741 the trustees, at Vernon's behest, divided Georgia into two counties, choosing Stephens as president of the northern half and tendering the other to Oglethorpe more as a sop to his vanity than for any profound political reason.[217] By the end of his tenure in Georgia, Oglethorpe had thus lost virtually all the great administrative powers which had been his during the past decade.

Although he lost his grip on other colonial affairs, Oglethorpe retained his post of Commissioner for Indian Affairs, which now became a vital question in the problem of colonial defence. As McCain asserts, "Colonel Oglethorpe was a master hand in winning the confidence and support of the red men."[218] As early as his first year in Georgia, he had pacified them, and his subsequent visits, thanks largely to Tomochichi, had found them faithful. The death of Tomochichi in October, 1739,[219] the renewed activities of the Spaniards, and the underhand machinations of certain South Carolinians[220] made it imperative for Oglethorpe to pay particular attention to this problem. Having held an Indian conference at Savannah in 1736, he now proposed to bind them closer by personal

---

[214]"Collections of the Georgia History Society". Volume II, pp. 87-162.

[215]Osgood, *op. cit.* Volume III, pp. 63-66.

[216]*Ibid.*, p. 52.

[217]*Ibid.*, pp. 42, 67-68; "Egmont Diary". Volume III, p. 169. December 19, 1740; p. 171. December 27, 1740.

[218]McCain, *op. cit.*, p. 80.

[219]"Colonial Records of Georgia". Volume IV. "Stephens' Journal", p. 428.

[220]"Egmont Diary". Volume III, p. 7. January 24, 1739. Citing a letter from Oglethorpe. October 7, 1738.

contact in their own environs. As the report of one of his rangers shows, Oglethorpe made a journey of three hundred miles into the interior in 1739, and during the next three crucial years rode periodically with his rangers to maintain the peace established years before with Tomochichi.[221] As the attitude of the Indians during the war indicated, the result was worth the effort.

Important as were its religious progress, its administrative problems and its Indian relations in this period, the vital factor in the life of Georgia was the war with Spain. For thirty years peace had reigned between England and the Continent, but illicit British trade with Spanish America and the consequent Spanish reprisals reopened the European conflict. The first Spanish attack on Georgia in 1737[222] had been followed by a formal claim of all Georgia by Giraldini, the Spanish Minister in London. Walpole now temporized and, to the agonizing fear of the trustees, used Georgia as a pawn in obtaining the convention of 1738 with Spain. Only the strong protests of the trustees "to keep Georgia out of the Spaniards' hands" prevented its transfer.[223] The convention proved void and Walpole's peace policy was brought to an end by the popular demand for a maritime war with Spain, a demand largely created by reputed Spanish cruelties, one of which gave the conflict its title of "The War of Jenkins' Ear". On October 23, 1739, war with Spain was officially declared.[224] The Colonial Office Papers in the Public Record Office are rich in official correspondence between the West Indian governors and those on the North American continent, all seeking the best means of defence against the marauding Spaniard[s].[225] Oglethorpe's advice was frequently sought for on him fell the greatest responsibility. Georgia, by virtue of both its proximity to Florida and its

---

[221]Mereness, N. D. "Travels in the American Colonies". New York. 1916. pp. 218-236. "A Ranger's Report of Travels with General Oglethorpe, 1739-1742." See also "Colonial Records of Georgia". Volume XXII, Part II, p. 214. Letter, author unknown. Charles Town. September 11, 1739.

[222]"Egmont Diary". Volume II, p. 376. March 23, 1737.

[223]*Ibid.*, Volume III, pp. 9-45, *passim.* January 24-March 25, 1739.

[224]*Ibid.*, Volume III, p. 86. October 23, 1739.

[225]See especially C.O. 23. Bahamas. Volumes 4 and 14; C.O. 37. Bermuda. Volume 13; and C.O. 137. Jamaica. Volume 56.

status in Spanish eyes as *terra irredenta*, was the logical point of first attack. In Georgia the military drama opened with a mutiny among the Gibraltar troops brought over by Oglethorpe. In this affair one hundred soldiers marched to his tent to demand full subsistence. Explaining the situation, he ordered them to their quarters, whereupon "two of them levelled their pieces at him and fired, the shot of one entirely missed him, but the other passed between his wig and cheek, and providentially missed him." One rebel was killed, another arrested, the mutiny was quelled, and Oglethorpe began his preparations for defence.[226] The mutiny had however had one good effect. The continual struggles of the trustees with Walpole for further parliamentary appropriations had discouraged him to the point where he saw "nothing but Destruction to the Colony unless some assistance be immediately sent us."[227] The mutiny aroused his fighting instinct and he described to a friend the difficulties which "rather animate than daunt me": "I am here in one of the most delightful Situations as any man could wish to be. A great number of Debts, empty Magazines, no money to supply them, Numbers of People to be fed, mutinous Soldiers to Command, a Spanish Claim & a large body of their Troops not far from us."[228]

The war in Georgia developed into an English attack on St. Augustine in 1740 and a Spanish riposte in 1742. Oglethorpe's visit to the Indians in 1739 had been followed by a slave insurrection in South Carolina, attributed to Spaniards, and a Spanish outrage on Amelia Island,[229] which was justified in their eyes by Oglethorpe's establishment of a fort in contested territory.[230] Having written to the trustees that "I have received the King's Commands to anoy [*sic*] the Spaniards and am

---

[226]"Egmont Diary". Volume III, p. 6. January 19, 1739; "Gentleman's Magazine". Volume IX. 1739. pp. 48 and 215.

[227]"Colonial Records of Georgia". Volume XXII, Part I, p. 283. Oglethorpe to the Trustees. October 19, 1738.

[228]*Ibid.*, p. 314. Oglethorpe to Alderman George Heathcote. Frederica. November 20, 1738.

[229]McCrady, Edward. "The History of South Carolina under the Royal Government, 1719-1776". New York. 1899. pp. 184-187; Osgood, *op. cit.* Volume III, pp. 503-504.

[230]Osgood, *op. cit.* Volume III, p. 502.

going to Execute them,"[231] Oglethorpe now conceived as a retaliatory measure, an attack on St. Augustine. Loyally aided by the South Carolinians, to whom their former object of hate was now a potential saviour, Oglethorpe proceeded in May, 1740, to the attack. In the words of Stevens, "the plans of Oglethorpe were eminently military and judicious; his valour was unimpeached; his zeal untiring, and his energy unexhausted,"[232] but the attack failed and the expedition returned without effecting its purpose.[233] Oglethorpe charged the South Carolinians with failure to co-operate in the crises, but this was successfully refuted[234] and a charge of incompetency in turn was hurled at the general.[235] The failure of this expedition affected Oglethorpe's health. As Stephens noted in his journal, the commander was "reduced to an extraordinary Weakness by a continual Fever" and "the Disappointment of Success (it is believed) now galled him, and too great Anxiety of Mind preyed upon him."[236] The fever continued for two months, but the spirit was still alive and it hastened his recovery.[237]

Well again, his executive troubles returned. Always the preparation for the attack which he knew must come; always the appeal for more support. The trustees, disturbed at his extravagance in military expenditures, failed him; the British government, none to anxious to save Georgia, failed him. In desperation he had instructed Verelst, the accountant for the trustees, to "raise money on all his estate, real and personal, without limitation of the sum, as also to employ all his salary from the Government for answering the bills he should draw on him for the service of the public." His providence was needed for South Carolina

---

[231]"Colonial Records of Georgia". Volume XXII, Part II, p. 217. Oglethorpe to the Trustees. Savannah. October 5, 1739.

[232]Stevens, op. cit. Volume I, p. 178.

[233]Osgood, op. cit. Volume III, pp. 504-507; McCrady, op. cit., pp. 196-229.

[234]South Carolina Historical Society Collections. Volume IV. "Report on the St. Augustine Expedition".

[235]McCrady, op. cit., pp. 224-229.

[236]"Colonial Records of Georgia". Volume IV. "Stephens' Journal, 1737-1740", p. 635.

[237]Ibid., p. 653.

had been unable to raise, on her own credit, the funds pledged towards the pay of the troops, and it was Oglethorpe who now personally supplied the money.[238] A second illness "through fatigue and vexation",[239] and the pronounced hostility of a subordinate officer by the name of Cook, who had served under him in the St. Augustine expedition, preceded the Spanish attack of 1742.[240]

Oglethorpe did not fear the enemy. His previous encounters had confirmed his views as to their ultimate impotency. In a letter to the trustees he wrote: "As God has been pleased hitherto to overcome all these oppositions, I think from thence we are much more likely to succeed than we were before we knew what opposition we were to receive."[241] Thus, when in the late spring of 1742, the Spanish expeditionary force arrived below Frederica, Oglethorpe was ready. The situation was now the reverse of that in 1740 and he made the most of it. With the defences in place if needed, Oglethorpe ambushed the enemy and utterly routed them in what McCain has called "the high watermark of his career".[242] The victorious commander celebrated the preservation of Georgia by ordaining that July 25, 1742, be set apart "as a day of public thanksgiving to Almighty God for His great deliverance in having put an end to the Spanish invasion."[243]

Although defeated in their attack on Georgia, the Spaniards remained an ever-present danger in Florida and Oglethorpe continued both his appeals for aid and his defensive measures. Dismayed by the utterly apathetic attitude of the British government, he now appealed directly to the Duke of Newcastle who, with his brother, Henry Pelham, had displaced Walpole in control of the Whig oligarchy. In a series of

---

[238]"Egmont Diary". Volume III, p. 146. June 2, 1740.

[239]*Ibid.*, p. 214. April 20, 1741.

[240]*Ibid.*, p. 213. April 13, 1741.

[241]"Collections of the Georgia Historical Society". Volume III. 1873. "Oglethorpe Letters", p. 113. Oglethorpe to the Trustees. April 28, 1741.

[242]McCain, *op. cit.*, p. 86; Osgood, *op. cit.*, Volume III, pp. 507-509.

[243]"Collections of the Georgia Historical Society". Volume III, p. 139. "Report on the Spanish Invasion", etc.; see also Tyerman, L. "George Whitefield". Volume II, p. 23.

remarkable letters he explained the vital importance of Georgia as a buffer state and portrayed the dire consequences of its conquest by Spain, the knowledge of which he wrote, "has made me expend my fortune and expose my person much more than by the strictest rules of duty I should have been obliged to." Praying that the frontier be properly protected, he refused to "be blamed if I dye in an unsuccessful defence of it for the being killed in one's duty is all that the bravest man or best officer that wants the necessary means of war, can do."[244] Receiving no reply and feeling that "my remaining in uncertainty may not only prove fatal to myself but very probably the consequence of it may be the loss of two or three Provinces,"[245] Oglethorpe renewed his appeals to Newcastle, explaining that "it was by the great Blessing of God that we defeated the Enemy" for "they had all Preparations, numbers, and time sufficient to have destroyed us and had I been as incredulous and as unprepared, they had in all human probability not only conquered Georgia, but both Carolinas, for the Negroes could have certainly revolted, and if the Spaniards had defeated us, they had nothing but what would have run from them." In measured words he boldly declared that "I would not trouble Your Grace with these Reflexions were not it necessary to prevent future ill Consequences by dear bought experience. I hope this good use may be made of a bad accident that it may give weight to the representations of those who are near danger and who can certainly perceive the danger and take the measures necessary for defence sooner than those at a distance can."[246] His efforts were in vain.

Despite the silence in Westminster Oglethorpe in March, 1743, made a further raid against St. Augustine.[247] From his Florida camp he informed Newcastle that "I should think myself inexcusable if I did not inform Your Grace of the dangerous scituation of His Majesty's Colo-

---

[244]"Collections of the Georgia Historical Society". Volume III, p. 124. Oglethorpe to the Duke of Newcastle. November 24, 1742.

[245]*Ibid.*, p. 126. Oglethorpe to Andrew Stone. November 24, 1742.

[246]"Collections of the Georgia Historical Society". Volume III, pp. 128-129. Oglethorpe to the Duke of Newcastle. January 22, 1743.

[247]Osgood, *op. cit.* Volume III, p. 510.

nies."[248] But St. Augustine refused to surrender, the expedition failed in its main purpose, and Oglethorpe returned to Georgia to ponder the situation. It was true that his defence of the colony had made him its idol,[249] but in Carolina his name was anathema.[250] At home the government, to be sure, had promoted him to the rank of Brigadier General,[251] but his mainstay on the Georgia Board, the Earl of Egmont, had resigned from the Council "partly by reason of my ill health" as he noted in his diary, "and partly from observing the ill behaviour of the Ministry and Parliament with respect to the colony."[252] In addition to this blow, Oglethorpe found that Lieutenant Colonel Cook had proceeded to London where, as Egmont notes, he brought charges against the general "of defrauding his regiment by making them pay for the provisions the Government sent them over gratis."[253] Oglethorpe faced the inevitable and, despondent at heart, turned toward England.

Departing with the blessings of his people in Georgia,[254] James Oglethorpe returned to England on September 28, 1743,[255] having given to the colony a decade of his best years and a fortune which, owing to parliamentary parsimony, he was well-nigh unable to replenish. A month later he was once more among his friends.[256] While awaiting the

---

[248]"Collections of the Georgia Historical Society". Volume III, p. 150. Oglethorpe to Newcastle. March 12, 1743.

[249]"Colonial Records of Georgia". Volume XXIII, p. 428. T. Causton to Verelst. Oxted, Georgia. November 16, 1742; p. 460. Jo. Dobell to the Earl of Egmont. Savannah. January 5, 1743. Volume XXIV, p. 27. T. Causton to Verelst. May 10, 1743; p. 106. Bolzius to Martyn. Ebenezer. September 15, 1743.

[250]"Egmont Diary". Volume III, p. 218. April 23, 1741. A kinder view is that found in "Colonial Records of Georgia". Volume XXIII, p. 532. Mr. Beaufain to the Earl of Egmont. Charlestown, S.C. March 6, 1743.

[251]Dalton, op. cit., p. 53; "Gentleman's Magazine". Volume XIII. 1743. p. 107.

[252]"Egmont Diary". Volume III, p. 265. July 7, 1742.

[253]Ibid., p. 266. August 23, 1742.

[254]"Colonial Records of Georgia". Volume XXIV, p. 106. Rev. Mr. Bolzius to Benjamin Martyn. Ebenezer. September 15, 1743.

[255]"Gentleman's Magazine". Volume XIII. 1743. p. 498.

[256]"Egmont Diary". Volume III, p. 275. October 28, 1743; p. 279. December 22, 1743.

court-martial he again besought Parliament for the advances he had made in the defence of Georgia. This time he was successful, for on March 20, 1744, Egmont recorded that "this day the House of Commons granted the sums expended by General Oglethorpe in defence of Georgia, amounting to above 60,000*l.* without any division. Sir Jo. Cotton, who was ever an enemy to the colony, desired to know what use the colony was of to England, which gave the General an opportunity of shewing that on the preservation of it depends that of all the northern provinces. He was well heard by the House."[257] In June he was tried at the Horse Guards by a Board of General Officers on a charge comprising nineteen articles. Sitting but two days, the Board passed on the charges, article by article, and, branding them as "false, malicious, and without foundation," acquitted Oglethorpe and ordered Cook to be dismissed from the service.[258] The triumph was complete and in August Oglethorpe wrote again to Newcastle, offering his services if needed for the protection of his beloved Colony.[259]

Oglethorpe continued his interest in the colony by an erratic attendance at Board meetings, where he maintained, however, his right of dissent from the accepted proceedings of the trustees.[260] The colony continued to struggle along under the trustees who, save for Egmont, Vernon and Oglethorpe, gave up well-nigh all interest therein. In July, 1742, the act prohibiting rum had been repealed;[261] on January 9, 1749, Oglethorpe attended his last Council meeting;[262] the next year the Anti-Slavery Law was repealed;[263] and in 1752 the colony, in accordance with its charter, reverted to the Crown. McCain has well defined the place of

---

[257]*Ibid.*, p. 293. March 20, 1744.

[258]*Ibid.*, p. 300. June 12, 1744; "Gentleman's Magazine". Volume XIV. 1744. p. 336.

[259]"Collections of the Georgia Historical Society". Volume III, p. 155. Oglethorpe to Newcastle. August 24, 1744.

[260]E.g., "Colonial Records of Georgia". Volume II, pp. 431, 445 and 489.

[261]*Ibid.*, Volume I, p. 55.

[262]*Ibid.*, Volume II, p. 490. On March 19, 1749, he attended his last board meeting. Volume I, p. 529.

[263]*Ibid.*, Volume I, p. 56.

Oglethorpe in these later days: "Had he been as interested after 1743 as he was when the work was first begun, he would have ranked with Vernon and Egmont in his attendance, and his right to the first place among the Trustees could hardly have been questioned. As it is, the position of honor assigned him is based on his activities during the first decade of the Trust."[264]

In a survey of Oglethorpe's life it may not be out of order to consider why his project, so ideal in purpose and character, should have failed. The answer lies within the question. It was too ideal. Channing accurately stated the case when he wrote: "Oglethorpe and his associates were actuated by the highest and most honorable motives; but their regulations were not conducive to the success of the enterprise." The limited size of farms in Georgia coupled with the prohibition of negro slave labour and the law of entail male, did not allow the Georgians to compete with the rich slaveholding landowners of Carolina, at whose expense in the loss of valuable lands and a lucrative fur trade, "Georgia fulfilled its mission as a 'buffer' colony."[265] On the other hand, the late Professor Egerton, who lauded the founding of Georgia as "noteworthy because it affords the first example of State-aided emigration as a remedy for distress at home," found its failure to be "no occasion for surprise. . . . The attempt to convert the unemployed into a kind of Roman Colony, who should both work and act as a frontier guard against the Indians, was foredoomed to failure."[266] As to Oglethorpe's part in the project McCain's conclusions were probably the most equable when he wrote that, although "it would have been better for the province if Oglethorpe had never gone to Georgia, . . . it is unlikely that any person could have been found who had the natural qualifications and the enthusiasm possessed by Oglethorpe."[267]

---

[264]McCain, *op. cit.*, p. 51.

[265]Channing, *op. cit.* Volume II, pp. 363-365. In accordance with Channing is C. Grant Robertson in his "England under the Hanoverians", p. 211.

[266]Egerton, H. E. "A Short History of British Colonial Policy", p. 160.

[267]McCain, *op. cit.*, pp. 96-97.

V

His return from Georgia marked the apex of Oglethorpe's career. The remainder was but an anti-climax. In September 15, 1744, after almost fifty years of celibacy, James Oglethorpe married Elizabeth, the only daughter of the late Sir Nathan Wright, Bart., of Cranham Hall, Essex,[1] gaining thereby not merely a charming spouse but also a large dower and the Essex estate. After a career which had led him to the Levant and across the Atlantic, the wanderer had found a home. The press, which of late had overlooked him, now broke forth again, this time in epithalamial verse.[2] But the happy bridegroom was not permitted to enjoy his new state in uninterrupted peace.

Charles Stuart, son of the Old Pretender, had decided to make one last desperate bid for Stuart restoration by an invasion of England through Scotland. Forgetting the Jacobite connexions of his youth, England called on James Oglethorpe to defend her against one who, if the Shaftoe narrative bears any truth, was his own nephew. In March, 1744, he was chosen "to have a commission for raising a regiment of hussars to defend the coasts",[3] and a year later was created Major-General.[4] By

---

[1]"Gentleman's Magazine". Volume XIV. 1744. p. 506. In its August issue, p. 451, this journal had erroneously reported his marriage to a Miss Sambrooke, a sister of the late Sir Jeremy Sambrooke, Bart. It seems evident that at this time Oglethorpe had his eye on the eligible heiresses.

[2]*Ibid.*, p. 558. October verse. "On the Marriage of General Oglethorpe".

[3]Toynbee, Mrs. Paget. "The Letters of Horace Walpole". Sixteen volumes. Oxford. 1903-1905. Volume II, p. 10. Horace Walpole to Horace Mann. March 1, 1744.

[4]March 31, 1745. Dalton, *op. cit.*, p. 53. Also "Gentleman's Magazine". Volume XV. 1745. p. 220.

November the news had spread that "the bucks, . . . to the number of twenty or thirty, have listed under a mad general—Oglethorpe,"[5] who thus converted a body of Yorkshire foxhunters into hussars[6] who, "on the march against the rebels, . . . made a fine appearance and do an honour to their King and country."[7] With them he took a body of his Georgia rangers.[8] Serving under Marshal Wade,[9] Oglethorpe pursued the rebels to Doncaster[10] and Manchester[11] where he won an engagement.[12] He now forced his way ahead of the rebels to join Wade at Chesterfield.[13] Sent thence with 500 horse[s] to join the Duke of Cumberland at Preston,[14] Oglethorpe's pursuit was halted at the battle of Clifton Moor, whence he turned with his horse to Carlisle.[15] Here he spent Christmas Day.[16] But his error in allowing the rebels to escape at Clifton Moor cost

[5]Hist. MSS. Com. Volume 61. Sixteenth Report. Lady Du Cane MSS. p. 77. Stephen Thompson to Vice-Admiral Medley. London. November 8, 1745.

[6]Toynbee, *op. cit.* Volume II, p. 140. Horace Walpole to Horace Mann. October 4, 1745.

[7]Hist. MSS. Com. Volume 32. Thirteenth Report. Appendix. Part VI. Sir William Fitzherbert MSS. p. 161. Letter of an unknown author. Morpeth. November 4, 1745.

[8]"Gentleman's Magazine". Volume XV. 1745, p. 624.

[9]Hist. MSS. Com. Volume 32. Thirteenth Report. Appendix. Part VI. Sir William Fitzherbert MSS. p. 165. John Billam to——. Sandbeck. December 7, 1745. See also Dalton, *op. cit.*, p. 53.

[10]*Ibid.*, p. 166.——to——. Doncaster. December 12, 1745.

[11]*Ibid.*, p. 169. John Holland to Dickenson Knight. Manchester. December 20, 1745.

[12]*Ibid.*, pp. 173-174. December 15, 1745. See also Toynbee, *op. cit.* Volume II, p. 162. Horace Walpole to Horace Mann. December 20, 1745.

[13]*Ibid.*, p. 175. Chesterfield. December 19, 1745.

[14]Hist. MSS. Com. Volume 38. Fourteenth Report. Appendix. Part IX. Trevor MSS. p. 138. Horatio Walpole to Robert Trevor. December 17/28, 1745.

[15]*Ibid.* Volume 55. MSS. in Various Collections. Volume VIII. The Honourable F. L. Wood Collection, p. 151.

[16]*Ibid.*, p. 155. For other references to Oglethorpe in this campaign, see pp. 108, 141 and 148.

him dearly. In the new year he was stricken off the staff of the Duke of Cumberland and exposed to the possibilities of a court-martial. Even his old friend, Egmont, regretfully noted that "he is an unfortunate man, his vanity and quarrelsomeness rendering him incapable to preserve the friendship of his acquaintance or make new friends, and every mouth is now open against him with a kind of satisfaction."[17] The prospective court-martial materialized in a trial set for September 29, 1746.[18] In October Horace Walpole, who had no great love for him, noting in a letter that courts-martial "are all the fashion now," remarked that "Oglethorpe's sentence is not yet public but it is believed not to be favourable," adding gratuitously that "he was always a bully, and is now tried for cowardice."[19] Contrary to Walpole's cherished hopes, and despite the overwhelming popularity of the Duke of Cumberland who brought the charges, Oglethorpe was acquitted, and on September 3, 1747, was promoted to be Lieutenant-General.[20] Although acquitted, this episode closed his active military career, although on February 22, 1765, he was commissioned a full General.[21] McCall, in his history of Georgia, asserts that in the American Revolution, a decade later, Oglethorpe, as senior general, was offered command of the British expeditionary force, which he declined on being refused the power to treat with the Americans.[22] This story is unsupported by evidence and it is reasonable to suppose that long ere this the last call had sounded and Oglethorpe had retired to civil life.

The colonist had returned; the Parliamentarian had retired; the soldier had stacked his arms; the man remained. Except for an appoint-

---

[17]"Egmont Diary". Volume III, pp. 312-313. January 18, 1746.

[18]Hist. MSS. Com. Volume 52. Fifteenth Report. Mrs. Frankland Russell Astley MSS. p. 346. Colonel Charles Russell to his Wife. London. August 21, 1746. Russell sat as a member of the court-martial.

[19]Toynbee, *op. cit.* Volume II, pp. 245-246. Horace Walpole to Horace Mann. October 14, 1746.

[20]Dalton, *op. cit.*, p. 53. See also the "Gentleman's Magazine". Volume XVII. 1747. p. 497.

[21]*Ibid.* See also the "Gentleman's Magazine". Volume XXXV. 1765. p. 147.

[22]McCall, H. "History of Georgia". Two volumes. 1818. Volume I, p. 325.

ment to the general committee of the Hospital for the Maintenance and
Education of exposed and deserted young Children,[23] and membership
in the committee to encourage the British fisheries,[24] Oglethorpe's later
years were spent among his friends in the literary circles of the century.
After his retirement from Parliament he renewed his friendship with
Marshal Keith in a letter wherein he exhibited his strong admiration for
Frederick the Great.[25]

In 1738 he had been one of the first properly to appraise and welcome Samuel Johnson on the appearance of his poem, "London".[26] In
fact Oglethorpe, then already a famous Englishman, proved a benefac-
tor to Samuel Johnson, the *inconnu*, who always acknowledged his obligation to him. While his beloved Georgia was passing through the first
paroxysms of the American Revolution, Oglethorpe was dining with
Johnson and Boswell[27]—having become acquainted with the latter in
1767 on the appearance of his "Account of Corsica"[28]—and listening to
one, Oliver Goldsmith, a mutual friend, singing Tony Lumpkin's song
in his new play "She Stoops to Conquer".[29] As in 1738 he sponsored
Johnson, so from 1765 on he encouraged Goldsmith and, when the latter
was attacked in the London papers, it was Oglethorpe who wrote to him
that "if a farm and a mere country scene will be a little refreshment from
the smoke of London, we shall be glad of the happiness of seeing you at
Cranham Hall."[30] To these friends Oglethorpe expounded his views on
current events, declaring that Parliament was too powerful,[31] and that

---

[23]"Gentleman's Magazine". Volume XIV. 1744. p. 277.

[24]*Ibid.* Volume XX. 1750. pp. 233 and 474.

[25]Hist. MSS. Com. Volume 8. Ninth Report. Lord Elphinstone Collection, pp.
229a-229b. Oglethorpe to Keith. Rotterdam. May 3, 1756.

[26]Boswell, *op. cit.*, p. 25.

[27]*Ibid.*, pp. 173-174, 221, 270 and 339.

[28]Boswell, *op. cit.*, p. 221 n.

[29]Prior J. "Life of Oliver Goldsmith, M.B." Two volumes. London. 1837. Volume II, p. 380.

[30]*Ibid.*, pp. 422-423. See also Dobson, *op. cit.*, pp. 28-29.

[31]Boswell, *op. cit.*, p. 339.

the House of Commons had usurped the power of the Nation's money and used it tyrannically. In his old age he returned to the Jacobite doctrine of divine right,[32] yet his sense of justice led him to attack "the Landed and Church Interest throughout the Kingdom" for designing to plunder the rich and imprison and starve the poor.[33]

Despite the death of his companion, Samuel Johnson, in 1784, Oglethorpe's last two years were as vigorous as any since "the Forty-Five". Having lost Goldsmith and Johnson, Oglethorpe now became the intimate friend of Hannah More, the poetess, who, quite enamoured of her "new admirer", told her sister he was "quite a peux chevalier, heroic, romantic, and full of the old gallantry."[34] In her presence he discussed politics with Edmund Burke who thought him the most extraordinary man of whom he had ever read, "for that he had founded the province of Georgia; had absolutely called it into existence, and had lived to see it severed from the empire which created it, and become an independent state."[35]

Horace Walpole, who in 1746 had called him a bully, was now his good friend, and wrote of him in 1783: "He is alert, upright, has his eyes, ears, and memory fresh. If you want any particulars of the last century, I can procure them."[36] At the end of two years, when Oglethorpe attended the sale at Christie's of Samuel Johnson's library, and made one of the first calls on John Adams, the first minister from the United States of America,[37] Walpole's opinion had not changed in the least: "His eyes, ears, articulation, limbs, and memory would suit a boy, if a

---

[32]*Ibid.*, pp. 434-435. 1783.

[33]Nichols, J. "Illustrations of the Literary History of the Eighteenth Century". Volume IV, pp. 522-523. Oglethorpe to George Scott. Cranham Hall. September 12, 1775.

[34]Roberts, William. "Memoirs of the Life of Mrs. Hannah More". Two volumes. London. 1836. Volume I, p. 256. Hannah More to her Sister, 1784.

[35]*Ibid.*, p. 287. Hannah More to her Sister. 1784.

[36]Toynbee, *op. cit.* Volume XII, p. 406. Horace Walpole to the Countess of Upper Ossory. Berkeley Square. February 18, 1783.

[37]Holmes, Abiel. "The Annals of America". Two volumes. Cambridge, Mass. 1829. Volume II, p. 530. Note XII. Letter of John Adams to Holmes. Quincy, Mass. November 14, 1807.

boy could recollect a century backwards. His teeth are gone; he is a shadow, and a wrinkled one; but his spirits and his spirit are in full bloom."[38]

Three months later Oglethorpe was dead and of no further interest to one who could write thus of Samuel Johnson: "How little will Dr. Johnson be remembered when confounded with the masses of authors of his own calibre!"[39] Yet the death of James Oglethorpe on June 30, 1785, removed one of whom Austin Dobson avowed: "He prosecuted Philanthropy in the spirit of a Paladin, rejoicing in the obstacles, the encounters, the nights sub Jove frigido."[40]

Thus closed a career which had been full of promise and replete with achievement; a career ushered in as a phoenix upon the smouldering embers of the Jacobite ruins of 1688, nurtured on Jacobite precepts and aspirations, exposed to treasonable temptations, evolved in Georgian Parliaments, matured in humanitarian movements, and brought to fruition in the expansion of the British Empire beyond the seas; the career of an imperial philanthropist.

In his delightful autobiography Edward Bok, the famous American editor, tells the story of his grandfather who created a garden isle out of a barren rock in the North Sea five miles from the coast of Holland. Here, while the father laboured, a courageous Dutch mother reared thirteen children. One day, when the children had grown to man's and woman's estate, the mother called them all together and told them the story of their father's successful struggle on "The Island of Nightingales". "And now," she said, "as you go out into the world I want each of you to take with you the spirit of your father's work, and each in your own way and place, to do as he has done: make you the world a bit more beautiful and better because you have been in it. That is your mother's message to you."

If on these pages is found the true record of his active life; if, though hasty, irascible and tactless as at times he admittedly was, the soul

---

[38]Toynbee, *op. cit.* Volume XIII, p. 259. Horace Walpole to Sir Horace Mann. Berkeley Square. April 8, 1785.

[39]*Ibid.*, p. 290. Horace Walpole to the Countess of Upper Ossory. Strawberry Hill. July 9, 1785.

[40]Dobson, *op. cit.*, p. 31.

of that man be understood; if, finally and above all, he did aught to procure and protect a nobler England and a greater Empire, then has James Edward Oglethorpe merited the fame he has attained, for his labours have made the world a bit more beautiful and better.

Index

hastened JEO's departure, 48; passage unpleasant, 48; colonists eulogize his vast humanity, 48; testimony of Bolzius, 49; break with Charles Wesley, 51; powerless to eject Jews, 51; and Wesley, 51; absence in England, 51; on return to England in 1734, 53; makes acquaintance of Court Zinzendorf, 53; David Nitschmann accompanies JEO on return to Georgia, 53; Zinzendorf persuades JEO to grant site for Moravians, 53; returns with three hundred immigrants, 53; laid out Frederica, 53-54; conferences with Spanish officers, 54; military considerations in policy, 54; power to draw bills on Trustees, 54; Trustees demand bills be presented to British Government, 54; prohibiting Negro slavery entails economic disadvantage, 55; appointed commissioner to grant licenses to trade with Indians, 55; conference with Chickasaws, 55; friendship with Tomochichi, 55; rumor of trafficking in furs, 56; first discord in JEO's colonial career, 57; sailed home in 1736, 57; four-hour conference with Egmont, 57; South Carolina appeal, 57; asks Parliament to grant £30,000, 57; Walpole seeks advice, 58; spent £3,000 of own money, 58; Walpole refuses power to raise militia, 58; commissioned general of the forces of South Carolina and Georgia, 58; Parliament grants £20,000, 59; refused commission, 59; Colonel Oglethorpe, 59; sails to Georgia for last time, 60; relations with religions in Georgia, 63; tightens law enforcement, 63; met by complaints, 63; curries favor with colonists, 63; hurt by Tailfer publication, 64; attacked by Thomas Stephens, 65; success in Indian affairs, 65-66; rides to Indian Country, 66; mutiny of troops put down, 67; undaunted by challenges, 67; conceives attack on Florida, 67-68; attack fails, 68; health affected, 68; recovers, 68; ambushes and defeats Spanish, 69; declares day of Thanksgiving, 69; appeals to Duke of Newcastle, 69-71; on possibility of Negro revolt, 70; another raid on St. Augustine, 70; returns again from Florida, 71; promoted in rank, 71; charges brought by Cook, 71; returns to England, 71; reimbursed by Parliament, 72; acquitted of charges, 72; continues interest in Georgia, 72; attends last council meeting, 72; place among the trustees, 73; why his scheme for Georgia failed, 73; marriage, 75; and the uprising of 1745, 75-77; courts-martial and acquittal, 77; further promotions, 77; later ideas on Parliament, 78-79; and Burke and More, 79; at sale of Johnson's library, 79; calls on John Adams, 79; death of, 80; summation of career, 80

Oglethorpe, Lewis, in Parliament, 2

Oglethorpe, Louisa Mary (Molly), 9

Oglethorpe, Sutton, 1

Oglethorpe, Theophilus, 1-2; loyalty to James II, 2; and "Glorious Revolution," 2; knighted, 2; flees to France, 2; returns to England, 2; takes oath to William, 2; elected to Parliament, 2; 40

Oglethorpe, Theophilus (son of Theophilus and E. Wall), in Parliament, 2, 6; leaves England for good, 9; baronetcy of, 10; Jacobite activity in Italy, 10-11, 12

Oglethorpe University, xxii

Oglethorpes, the, xx, xxi; in Civil War, 1; in Yorkshire, 1; loyalty to Stuarts, 9-10; continued Jacobitism, 11-13

Oxford, (city of), ix-x, xii, xiii